HIGH ST
GIVING

HIGH STREET GIVING

Getting support for local charities from high street shops and other businesses

by Dr Stephen Humble

Published by the Directory of Social Change

HIGH STREET GIVING

by Dr Stephen Humble

cover design by Beverley Tattersfield

First published 1990
Published by the Directory of Social Change
© Directory of Social Change

Typeset by Kerry Robinson
Printed in Britain by Biddles of Guildford

ISBN 0 907164 536

Directory of Social Change, Radius Works, Back Lane, London NW3 1HL

CONTENTS

INTRODUCTION

This book is by and large about company giving on a small scale to local charities and branches of larger charities, and how they should set about persuading local companies to give to them. It is the first ever survey of local support by companies. It includes well over one hundred companies which are represented in one form or another at the High Street and local level.

Two other guides to company giving published biannually by the Directory of Social Change – Major Companies and their Charitable Giving and A Guide to Company Giving – deal with applications from charities to head o‴ices of companies. The idea behind this book is that there is plenty of opportunity for local charities to gain support, in cash and in kind, from companies in their own areas.

Which companies have been included? The largest were those, taken from The Times 1000 list of the world's top companies, which have retailing outlets in the High Street or were known to have some other form of local presence. To this list were added companies that have local representation and a meritorious policy on charitable support, and companies with local representation that are not large and whose policy on charitable giving was not known as particularly outstanding.

Each entry in the book starts with details of the company's head office address and telephone number. Next, we describe how the company is represented locally and what it does. This is followed by a general statement of the company's policy on charitable support, including the latest year's cash donations to charities. All this serves to set the scene for the section on what the company does to support charities locally, and what a local charity might expect to receive if it approached the local branch for support.

The involvement of staff in the company with local charities can be very important, and any history of staff charitable activity is described. A final miscellaneous section deals with the company's reactions to approaches from charities, the name of the head office contact and any other relevant information.

There has been in recent years a great deal of growth of interest in support from 'for-profit' organisations to 'not-for-profit' ones. Whether there has been a commensurate increase in actual support is hard to tell. Possibly not. The general feeling in the voluntary sector appears to be that though there has been some growth in UK company support, it does not meet the aspirations, even the realistic aspirations, of those working for voluntary groups. And it certainly does not meet their needs. Nor does the level of company support match that achieved in the USA.

But awareness on both sides of the fence, for-profit and not-for-profit, is growing, and nowadays many administrative staff in company headquarters know what you are talking about when you ask questions about their policy on 'giving'.

There are some do's and don'ts in approaching companies which arise from the compilation of this book. The general principle to remember is that most companies want to help where they can. The directors are only too well aware that their profits come from the the local communities in which they are based. So even the apparently most hard-headed of firms usually has a soft centre. And even where they do not, it does no harm to remind them that in the local community, people are doing worthwhile things for free. Persist, and many will eventually yield.

Some companies do not mind making public their policies on charitable support. They believe that this informs a charity making an approach, as well as weeding out inappropriate requests from charities. Other companies are more coy about their giving, perhaps in the hope that this will depress the number of requests they receive. Do not be put off. Most companies and their branches find it hard to fend off all requests. Some need gentle persuasion, and enlightenment.

But, and this is a big 'but', do not go asking for and expecting an immediate, positive and large response. Cultivate the managers of your local companies. This means that, initially, you should do a bit of research on them. First of all, find out exactly what their names and titles are. There is nothing more damaging than getting those wrong in a first approach.

If you are serious about getting support and developing a long-term relationship with the company, wherever possible, check with the company's head office what regional organisation the company has. Sometimes, local managers are responsible not directly to the head office, but indirectly through a regional manager. Sometimes, it is the regional office which will hold the local budget for charitable support.

Don't ask for support straightaway, unless it is something quite modest you want. Get to know the manager. If possible, flatter him or her. For example, get them to open your visitors' day or draw your raffle prize. Give them an opportunity to get to know your voluntary group or charity. Then ask for a donation or sponsorship, or whatever it is you need. If they don't have the discretion to respond to your request, they can often put forward a recommendation to a regional or head office.

Do your research, too, on the staff involvement at the local branch level. The larger local staff associations will have their own charitable activities, sometimes organised by the staff themselves and sometimes organised through the company. But even if there is no actual structure for staff charitable activity, it pays to have some connection with an individual member of staff, for example, as a volunteer or member of your management committee. Charitable appeals often fall on stony ground because the charity has no known connection with a member of staff.

Don't let the fact that the company has 'adopted' a particular charity and picked it out for major or high profile support put you off. Often, companies have enough room to give to a range of organisations, even where they consider that one merits special attention. You have to start somewhere and get a foot through the door. Perhaps one day your charity will be adopted.

Never, ever, make an appeal to a company, if you are a local branch of a charity, without checking first with your charity's head office. Top of the list of companies' pet hates in dealing with appeal letters is the number they receive from branches of national charities which they are already supporting, or which they have already turned down. Equally, if they support you at a local level, they might then decide not to make a much larger donation to your charity's head office. On the other hand, if it is support in kind that you are after, it may be an advantage that the head office of the company is supporting the head office of your charity with a cash donation. This is something you could mention in your approach to the local branch of the company.

Almost as unpopular with companies is the circular letter. A constant theme in advice on charitable appeals which cannot be repeated too often is: **do not send circular letters.** The circular letter is the one piece of paper in the shoal of appeals companies receive from charities that goes straight from envelope to waste paper bin.

Don't make it easy for companies to turn you down. For a successful 'beyond the bin' response, try to make your approach as personal as possible, in person if possible. Telephone if necessary. And only write a letter as a last resort. Always be prepared to follow up your approach with a copy of your charity's latest annual accounts.

Keep in mind the fact that cash support from companies to local charities is limited. So do not be disappointed if all you get is a gift of, say, £25 or a gift voucher. Build on what you are given. Tell the company what their gift purchased for your charity. Above all, find some excuse to keep in touch. It can lead to bigger and better things in the future.

The amount of discretion given to local managers varies greatly from company to company. Some firms are highly decentralised, whilst others do not allow their managers, in the words of the appeals director of a prominent and very profitable British company, 'to give away a penny piece'. So be prepared for a varied reaction.

Some large chains are inclined to allow a certain degree of cash or in-kind support. But in all cases it is far easier to obtain in-kind support of little or no value to the company, but which can be of tremendous value to the recipient. For example, companies may be able to donate furniture and equipment which are being replaced; surplus lines or outdated stock may be ripe for the picking; the company may be an ideal location for positioning a collecting box or two, or for organising a collection on the company forecourt (where no licence is required); and donations in cash and in kind can often be lost as 'stock shrinkage' or under general budget heads.

When purchasing on behalf of your charity, voluntary group or whatever, always ask for a discount. A few companies have a policy of allowing discounts to charities. And many more can be persuaded. If you are offered a discount, try to negotiate a bigger discount. After all, you are using hard-won charitable funds to make the purchase, and it is worthwhile trying to make the best deal you can. This will make the task of your fund-raising that much easier, as any funds that you raise will go that much further. You can even mention this when you are negotiating the level of discount.

Remember the difference between manufacturer, wholesaler and retailer, and the different costs that each bears. For example, in seeking a donation of free travel tickets for your charity's raffle prize, a travel agent will think twice, compared with an airline, about giving away 'plane tickets, simply because the cost of these to the agent is much greater.

Note the important difference between support and sponsorship, and the different budgets that companies operate in this area. Many companies are eager to find suitable sponsorship deals, even at local level, which will yield them valuable publicity. The rules of many building societies preclude them from giving directly, but they are still able to enter sponsorship arrangements. And don't underestimate the return you and your charity are expecting. Normal publicity and advertising cost companies a lot of money. Publicity coupled with doing a charity a good turn is very good publicity indeed for a company.

Local publicity never hurts, and you and your voluntary group may be a valuable source of local publicity for a company. Invite the local manager to draw your raffle prizes and turn the event into a photo call. You may earn him or her brownie points with the company head office, and get that first opening you have been looking for into asking for a donation.

Don't ask for inappropriate donations. For example, the breweries turn down scores of requests from school parent associations because they do not want to be considered providing for the needs of school children out of profits from alchohol.

Looking beyond the major chains, there are many smaller companies and family firms which have an explicit policy of only giving locally. There are also small shops and small local businesses which could be persuaded to give, if asked. None of these is covered in this book. You will have to rely on your own local knowledge of your area and your own contacts. But the small local firms do present a tremendous opportunity. Of those which do not as yet give locally, cultivate them and give them an opportunity to build links with local voluntary groups and charities.

Last but not least, do not forget that out of acorns, oak trees grow! And in the same way, small donations can lead eventually to large scale support. The very best of luck with the approaches you make to your local companies.

Dr Stephen Humble
January 1990

Companies included in this book

We have included companies with large chains of retail outlets and a selection of larger corporate givers with a specific local emphasis in their giving policy. If there are companies or retail chains which you would like to see included in the next edition of this book, please write to Dr Stephen Humble, the editor of High Street Giving, at the address below.

Special offer to readers

This is the first edition of this book. We hope to update it regularly. To do this, we hope to incorporate readers' experiences and local examples of good practice. If there is anything relevant you think you can contribute, please let us know. If we use the information, we will send you a free copy of the next edition when it is published. Please send any information, in as much detail as you can, to Dr Stephen Humble, Directory of Social Change, Radius works, Back Lane, London NW3 1HL. Thank you.

ABBEY NATIONAL PLC

Abbey House
Baker St
London NW1 6XL   *Tel 071-4 86 5555*

LOCAL ORGANISATION. One of Britain's largest building societies with more than 1,000 local branches nationwide. Also runs the chain of Cornerstone estate agencies (406 branches by the end of 1988).

POLICY. During 1988 the Group made cash contributions totalling £188,000 to UK charitable organisations. No contributions were made for political purposes.

LOCAL GIVING. Many appeals are forwarded to head office. It is possible for charities making local approaches to be given funding or support of some kind through Abbey National sponsorship, but this requires a business return to the Group. Branches are regionally based, and the regional offices have a limited budget for sponsorship.

GIVING IN KIND. The Group has been known to give equipment it no longer needed.

STAFF ACTIVITIES. Payroll giving and a matched giving scheme, whereby the Group matches pound for pound charitable contributions from staff up to a certain maximum, are being considered. The group sometimes makes arrangements to act as a collecting point for large appeals, eg in the case of Y Care International crisis appeals. But the Group does not promote particular charities amongst staff. Very occasionally, staff are seconded to voluntary groups.

OTHER INFORMATION. Contact should be made at head office through the Secretariat Dept.

ALLIANCE AND LEICESTER BUILDING SOCIETY

Hove Administration
Hove Park
Hove
East Sussex BN3 7AZ   *Tel 0273 775454*

LOCAL ORGANISATION. 410 building society and estate agency branches throughout the UK.

POLICY. During 1988 the Society made donations for charitable purposes amounting to £28,126. Donations from this budget are decided at 'very senior management level'. The budget is expected to be at the £30,000 level for 1989.

LOCAL GIVING. The Society is able to help on a greater scale from its marketing budget through sponsoring charities and charity related work, but this must yield a business return to the Society. It has a number of sponsorship programmes in Sussex and Leicestershire where there are large administrative offices. Regional controllers also have limited local budgets for purposes of sponsorship.

GIVING IN KIND. Local branches are sometimes able to give window space to publicise a local charity or act as a collecting point for a particular appeal.

STAFF ACTIVITIES. There is a staff payroll giving scheme.

OTHER INFORMATION. There are plans in hand to tie up with a national charity. In the past, the Society has supported Y Care International with its crisis appeals and acted nationally as a collecting point.

ALLIED BREWERIES

107 Station Rd
Burton-upon-Trent   *Tel 0283 45320*

LOCAL ORGANISATION. A trading group of companies owned by Allied Lyons (see separate entry). Includes brewery operations in Warrington, Leeds, Wrexham and Romford. Also depots, pubs and retail shops across the country as well as European operations in Rotterdam, etc.

POLICY. Support from the Allied Breweries group to charities is a 'complicated affair'. The parent company has its own policy and a large budget for support. Allied Breweries is permitted a budget by the parent company, running currently at some £30,000. Donations are, however, often not made in the name of Allied Breweries but come from the locus of operations, eg the local brewery. The Group head office in Burton also has a budget for charitable support. £5,000 of this went to the Lichfield cathedral appeal which was an appeal fairly local to the Group's centre of operations. Giving from the group's head office normally goes to charities in the fields of education, the elderly, hospices, hospitals and the cancer charities.

LOCAL GIVING. The budget for charitable support is divided up currently into 6 separate budgets of £4,000 each for each of the operating divisions of the Group.

OTHER INFORMATION. The Group provides pump priming money for charitable appeals and looks to sponsorship-type events. For example, it provided finance for the ITV Skol telethon which itself raised of the order of £1.4 million. The Burton office receives an average of three or four appeals each day. Contact: Mr Olphin, Company Secretary.

ALLIED LYONS PLC

156 St John St
London EC1 1AR   *Tel 071-253 9911*

LOCAL ORGANISATION. A large group represented locally across the UK through retailing outlets, mainly public houses and Victoria Wine shops. Brewery operations in various locations, including Joshua Tetley (Leeds), Allied Breweries (Burton-on-Trent) and Ansells (Birmingham). See separate entries for operating companies.

POLICY. A large charitable programme of donations of some £400,000 in 1988, the bulk of which goes to the Allied Lyons Charitable Trust. Contributions to charities are broadly spread. Head office gives to national, regional and local charities in the fields of social welfare, the arts, environment, education and science as well as enterprise agencies.

LOCAL GIVING. The operating companies each have their own smaller charitable budgets, and charities with a local connection with operating companies are advised to apply to them.

OTHER INFORMATION. The head office contact is Mr Neil Skinner, Assistant Company Secretary.

ANSELLS LTD

Tunbridge House
Aldridge Rd
Perry Barr
Birmingham B42 2TZ   *Tel 021-344 4567*

LOCAL ORGANISATION. Brewery operation in the West Midlands with public houses in the whole of the West Midlands, Staffordshire and Hereford and Worcestershire. Part of Allied Lyons (see separate entry).

POLICY. Has a small charitable budget which is separate from the parent company.

LOCAL GIVING. Obviously favours charities in its areas of operation.

GIVING IN KIND. The Company donates such products as beer and lager for raffles. It does not donate alchohol to support children's and youth charities, nor for school fetes.

OTHER INFORMATION. The Company begins looking at such things as charitable support in March of each year. It favours support to charitable events where sponsorship is involved, resulting in some publicity for the company. Contact should be made through the Marketing Dept.

ARGOS (See BAT Industries.)

ARGYLL GROUP PLC

Argyll House
Millington Rd
Hayes
Middlesex UB3 4AY   *Tel 081-848 8744*

LOCAL ORGANISATION. 247 Safeway and 84 Lo-Cost stores nationwide, and 184 Presto stores in the North.

POLICY. Cash charitable donations currently stand at about £100,000 annually. Appeals are treated individually and there is no set general policy. A few covenants to charities are made, organised from head office. For the first time, one national charity, St John Ambulance, is the main recipient. This policy will continue for two years and will then be reviewed.

LOCAL GIVING. Appeals are normally referred to head office. Small, local appeals are usually steered through district managers who will give a recommendation or otherwise and send positive recommendations to head office. But it is up to local managers if they want to give some small support to local charities in the form of a prize for a raffle, either in cash or in kind.

STAFF ACTIVITIES. Many stores have favourite local charities which they support. There is no secondment of staff.

OTHER INFORMATION. Contact should be made in writing at least one month in advance if support is being sought for a local charity event. For sponsorship, contact should be made with the Public Relations Dept at head office. Otherwise the head office contact is Mr J P Kinch, Company Secretary.

ASDA GROUP PLC

Asda House
Southbank
Gt Wilson St
Leeds LS11 5AD   *Tel 0532 435435*

LOCAL ORGANISATION. 130 stores nationwide. The Company is presently concentrating its expansion in the South.

POLICY. Selected national charities are adopted for fund raising purposes. £1.25 million was raised for the NSPCC and Help the Aged in 1988 through company, staff and customer contributions. The NSPCC was the Company's charity of the year in 1988 in England and Wales. Cash donations amounted in 1988 to £0.3 million (£0.2 million in 1987).

LOCAL GIVING. All requests are dealt with by head office. Store managers have a small annual budget for charitable giving. Local sponsorship events are encouraged and are part of company policy. For example, in 1988 Asda sponsored a Merseyside marathon, raising £50,000 for Childline. Events, including holiday schemes for youngsters, have been planned in some 50 locations for the coming year.

GIVING IN KIND. Any request is dealt with by head office. Sometimes vouchers can be provided.

STAFF ACTIVITIES. Fund raising by staff is encouraged. There are one or two secondments at present to Business in the Community. The staff are actively involved in supporting charities and the Company operates a matched giving scheme, matching cash contributions by staff to charities.

OTHER INFORMATION. The head office contact is Trevor Greenwood, Head of Public Relations.

AUGUSTUS BARNETT

North Woolwich Rd
Silvertown
London E16 2BN   *Tel 071-476 1477*

LOCAL ORGANISATION. Nationwide retailers of alchoholic wines and spirits etc with outlets numbered in the hundreds. Part of Bass Group (see separate entry).

POLICY. Operates within more or less the same policy guidelines as Bass, the parent group. The Company 'does try to help charities where it can'.

LOCAL GIVING. The Company is organised on a regional basis and assistance to charities may be considered by regional managers. Local managers do take an active role in supporting charitable work in various ways.

OTHER COMMENTS. Policy on charitable work is the responsibility of Mr Quaratan, the Managing Director.

AUSTIN REED GROUP PLC

103 Regent St
London W1A 2AJ   *Tel 071-734 6789*

LOCAL ORGANISATION. Retailer and manufacturer of clothes in outlets across the country and overseas. 42 outlets in the UK and two in Holland. Eight shops trade in the US under the name of Cashmeres of Scotland. The Company has traditional connections with Yorkshire.

POLICY. Donating is largely confined to the staff charities in the clothing trade, though there are one or two other donations made. During 1988 £22,436 was donated to charities.

LOCAL GIVING. Retail outlets normally pass appeals to head office.

OTHER INFORMATION. An 'awful amount' of charitable appeals are received by the company. The head office contact is Mr D M Anderson, Finance Director, who has an overview on charitable appeals.

B & Q

Eastleigh
Southampton   *Tel 0703 256256*

LOCAL ORGANISATION. Part of Kingfisher PLC (see separate entry). 236 branches in the UK retailing DIY and home goods.

POLICY. Local managers are generally requested to pass on appeals to head office.

LOCAL GIVING. A small budget is allocated to each branch for support to local charities. Demand on this budget can be heavy and often it is a case of 'first come, first served' since it is difficult to tell between deserving causes. One local manager reports that his budget for the six-month period is normally used up within one month and that a ten-fold increase in the budget would not suffice.

GIVING IN KIND. Local giving is invariably giving in kind, eg wallpaper, paint, tiles, lighting. Local hospitals are a great source of demand.

OTHER INFORMATION. A lot of requests come simply from people who come into the stores. The head office contact is Mr Peter Milne, Marketing Services Controller.

BAA PLC

130 Wilton Rd
London SW1V 1LQ   *Tel 071-834 9449*

LOCAL ORGANISATION. BAA's core business is the ownership and operation of airports. Through its subsidiaries at Heathrow, Gatwick, Stansted (see separate entries), Glasgow, Edinburgh, Prestwick and Aberdeen (see entry under Scottish Airports), the company handles 70% of UK passenger traffic and 85% of air cargo. It also manages Exeter, Southampton, Southend and Biggin Hill airports on behalf of their owners.

POLICY. BAA's charitable donations up to the end of March 1989 amounted to £193,000.

LOCAL GIVING. Each of the local airports has a small charitable budget for giving principally to local charities.

STAFF ACTIVITIES. Staff at the local airports do get involved in charity fund raising, and staff may also be involved and organised according to the department or airport terminal in which they work.

OTHER INFORMATION. Appeals through head office should be routed in the first instance through the Company Secretary's office. Local contacts at each airport are quoted under each entry.

BAT INDUSTRIES PLC

Windsor House
50 Victoria St
London SW1H 0NL

Tel 071-222 7979

LOCAL ORGANISATION. One of the largest companies based in the UK with international and local operations. Local operations in the UK are as follows: tobacco manufacturing with factories in Southampton and Liverpool; Wiggins Teape paper merchants with six paper mills and five factories spread across the country; Argos with a nationwide network of 231 catalogue showrooms; insurance services provided by Eagle Star (London head office) and Allied Dunbar (Swindon, Wiltshire, head office). At the time of going to press, BAT was under threat of a takeover bid and it is predicted that, regardless of the outcome, some of BAT's operating companies will be sold off.

POLICY. In 1988 payments by the Group for charitable purposes amounted to £2,030,000 which included £1,068,000 for various charitable projects operated by Allied Dunbar. Payments were made to various foundations and trusts concerned with management education, research, student welfare and the arts. Payments included £187,500 to the Health Promotion Research Trust, sponsored by the tobacco industry.

LOCAL GIVING. The Group is very devolved and giving to local charities is part and parcel of the Group's policy. Support from Group companies falls into two broad categories: donations to charities and support for community-based projects. But charitable donations are no longer the main channel of the Group's corporate giving. Their place is being taken over by wider-ranging support for community projects addressing the problems of the inner cities, unemployment and training.

For example, BAT Industries is heavily involved in support for the Brunswick Enterprise Centre, Liverpool. (It gave £1.1 million towards the cost of conversion of the buildings). The Brixton Enterprise Centre in South London has also received heavy support. Allied Dunbar, based in Swindon, is very involved in supporting charities in its region as well as nationwide. In the health field, with the closure of large hospitals for the mentally ill, Allied Dunbar has committed at least £1 million over a five year period to the development of facilities for sufferers and their families. Funds are also going under the auspices of the National Schizophrenia Fellowship to establish regional offices and workers across the country to support sufferers.

STAFF ACTIVITIES. There is an extensive programme of secondment of staff. There is also a matched giving scheme whereby the Group pledges to match pound for pound cash donations of staff to charities up to a maximum limit. Allied Dunbar in particular has a detailed and far-reaching policy on staff involvement in charities.

OTHER COMMENTS. Because of the diverse nature of the Group it is not possible to list all the addresses of the operating companies and their plants. Further information is available from Ms Susan Fisher, Corporate Information Manager, at head office (ext 3256).

BANK OF SCOTLAND GROUP

PO Box No 5
The Mound
Edinburgh EH1 1YZ   *Tel 031-442 7777*

LOCAL ORGANISATION. A clearing bank with outlets principally in Scotland and the major cities of England. Also runs amongst others the Bank of Wales and the British Linen Bank. Charitable donations amounted in 1988 to £313,500. No contributions were made for political purposes.

POLICY. The Bank favours charities that are based in Scotland since it considers English charities have greater access to companies in the South East and the rest of England. It deals with appeals as they come in and policy varies from year to year. The policy is 'reactive rather than proactive' and appeals are considered individually on their merits.

LOCAL GIVING. Branch managers have a small amount of discretion about direct support to local charities and may give of the order of £50-100. Above these amounts appeals should be sent to head office.

STAFF ACTIVITIES. As is common with banks, staff are heavily involved with local charities in such matters as accounts etc. There is a staff payroll giving scheme but no matched giving scheme.

OTHER INFORMATION. Contact at head office should be made through the Executive Office.

BARCLAYS BANK PLC

Community Enterprise Dept
PO Box 256
Fleetway House
25 Farringdon St
London EC4A 4LP   *Tel 071-489 1995*

LOCAL ORGANISATION. One of the big four banks with just under 3,000 High St branches across the country. Offices worldwide in excess of 4,000 in some 80 countries.

POLICY. Currently contributing some £9 million annually, as reckoned by the Bank, to the voluntary sector in cash or assistance of some kind. This sum includes donations made to national charities, activities by the Bank to support employment programmes, as well as secondment of staff (about 100 at present) to voluntary groups. One percent of profits to the community is the Bank's target figure. National donations receive special consideration if the work is in the field of education or medicine, or whose aim is to improve the quality of life of young people or those who are aged, handicapped or disadvantaged. Donations are also made for conservation work.

LOCAL GIVING. A 'very small part' of the total budget is allocated to the Bank's regional offices across the UK for local giving. If an appeal for a purely local project was received by head office, this would usually be passed to the relevant regional office for consideration. Similarly, if an appeal was received by a local bank manager, providing it met the internal criteria for consideration laid down by the Bank and carried the recommendation of the local manager, then it would be referred to the regional office and dealt with sympathetically. One of the important criteria is that normally, where the Bank is supporting a national charity from central funds, then it would not recommend a donation locally or regionally. Regional offices are quite at liberty to ask for a greater allocation of funds if demand is justified.

STAFF ACTIVITIES. Secondment of Bank staff to charities includes secondment to local groups. Secondment is organised from head office. A lot of staff are involved with charity work. The Bank operates a matching grant scheme whereby for every amount donated by a member of staff, Barclays matches it pound for pound, up to a maximum of £500 currently.

OTHER INFORMATION. Local sponsorship, from a separate budget, may also be given for such things as local theatres, festivals, school events, sporting activities, concerts, exhibitions and agricultural shows. Contact at head office should be made in the first instance through the Community Affairs Dept (see address above).

BASS PLC

30 Portland Place
London W1N 3DF   *Tel 071-637 5499*

LOCAL ORGANISATION. Brewing, drinks, pub retailing and leisure group. (See separate entries for Augustus Barnett off-licences, Crest Hotels and Coral racing).

POLICY. Some £650,000 in charitable donations in the last financial year, nearly half of which was channelled through the Bass Charitable Trust.

LOCAL GIVING. The Group does not donate to local appeals except where it has a company presence. Operating companies have their own policies on charitable donations, within set limits.

STAFF ACTIVITIES. Charities supported by members of staff are looked on favourably.

OTHER INFORMATION. Head office contact in the first instance through Mrs Jill de Wardener, Secretary to the Chairman.

BEJAM (See Iceland Bejam.)

BENTALLS PLC
Wood St
Kingston upon Thames KT1 1TX   *Tel 081-546 1001*

LOCAL ORGANISATION. Department store operator with the main store at Kingston upon Thames and branches at Ealing, Worthing, Bracknell, Tunbridge Wells and Tonbridge.

POLICY. Contributions in 1989 to UK charitable organisations amounted to £19,328 with an additional contribution of £2,000 to the Conservative Party. Appeals are generally dealt with at head office. Local organisations more than national charities are favoured. The general policy is to try to give to a spread of deserving causes.

LOCAL GIVING. Local general managers may have some limited funds and certain discretion over appeals. Stores will sometimes contribute to local fairs, bazaars and other fund raising events.

OTHER INFORMATION. The Rowan Bentall Charitable Trust has been specifically established to deal with contributions to registered charities. Contact at head office should be made initially through the Company Secretary, Mr John Ryan.

BIRMINGHAM MIDSHIRES BUILDING SOCIETY

PO Box 81
35-49 Lichfield St
Wolverhampton WV1 1EL   *Tel 0902 710710*

LOCAL ORGANISATION. Some 140 branches, mainly in the North West, Midlands, South West, and some in the South East.

POLICY. In 1988, donations were made to 43 individual charities, within the communities in the main areas of operation, amounting in total to £3,770 (£2,860 in 1987). The Society does not make contributions for political purposes. The 1989 budget is already allocated. There is a charities committee which considers every appeal on its merit.

LOCAL GIVING. The Society tends to favour the smaller charities in its areas of operation. It tends to avoid the large national charities.

GIVING IN KIND. Some local branches do give the odd item for such things as raffles for charity (eg a bottle of wine).

STAFF ACTIVITIES. There are staff charitable appeals.

OTHER INFORMATION. The Marketing Dept deals with sponsorship where the Society would be looking for a business return for its involvement with a particular charity.

BLUE ARROW PLC

31 Worship St
London EC2A 2DX
                                        Tel 071-638 7788

LOCAL ORGANISATION. National and international employment services company represented at local level through Brook St Bureaux, with some 100 High St branches nationwide.

POLICY. According to the last available accounts for the year ending October 1988, the Company made charitable donations of £420,000 and £5,000 was donated to the Conservative Party. A Charity Committee meets at the beginning of each year. All funds are presently utilised and appeals should be sent to the Company Secretary's office at the end of the year. There is a policy of giving to medical training, medical research and the relief of poverty. The Company also runs a Community Affairs Programme to assist young people and the unemployed in the inner cities.

LOCAL GIVING. Appeals are usually passed to head office via branches and regional managers. There is no harm in trying local branches but support will be limited to such things as helping sponsor local charity magazines etc.

OTHER INFORMATION. Appeals to head office should be directed in the first instance to the Company Secretary's office.

BRISTOL AND WEST BUILDING SOCIETY

Broad Quay
Bristol BS99 7AX
                                        Tel 0272 294271

LOCAL ORGANISATION. An extensive network of some 160 branches, mainly in Southern England. Also branches in Scotland.

POLICY. In support of various educational, medical and other organisations, charitable donations totalling £9,758 were made during the past year by the Society and its subsidiary companies. According to the Society, with the restrictions placed on charitable donations by building societies, small donations only can be made. There is a quarterly meeting at which all applications are considered in order to achieve giving on an equitable basis. Some funds are directed through the Charities Aid Foundation in order to spread giving.

LOCAL GIVING. Branch managers would normally send appeal letters to head office. The Society tends to support charities in its main geographical areas of operation.

STAFF ACTIVITIES. The Society operates a Give As You Earn Scheme. Staff are able to nominate charities for consideration. It is not the Society's policy to promote particular charities. Staff are involved in fund raising events for local charities.

BODY SHOP INTERNATIONAL PLC

Hawthorn Rd
Wick
Littlehampton
West Sussex BN17 7LR   *Tel 0903 717107*

LOCAL ORGANISATION. Well over 100 shops nationwide and growing. Over 250 shops in 34 overseas countries. The Group originates, produces and sells naturally-based skin and hair products and related items through its own shops and through franchised outlets.

POLICY. Very largely directed to the environment and community enterprise, though policy is continually evolving due to the fast growth of the Company. A new system is being created whereby franchisees pay royalties toward charitable donations.

LOCAL GIVING. Shops, as opposed to franchises, are given a small budget for charitable giving.

GIVING IN KIND. Gift baskets of company products are sometimes donated. Head office usually deals with these donations.

STAFF ACTIVITIES. Shop staff do engage in fund raising efforts. There is a particular effort aimed at raising money for a 'boys' town' in India where some Body Shop products are made.

OTHER INFORMATION. A small Environmental and Community Projects Department exists at head office, dealing with a variety of charity matters, including overseas.

THE BOOTS COMPANY PLC

1 Thane Rd West
Nottingham NG2 3AA   *Tel 0602 50611*

POLICY. Charitable donations last year totalled over £600,000. Health, education and young people are favourite areas though giving is widely distributed. Boots does not adopt particular charities, though it did provide support to the NSPCC when it was known to be in financial difficulty.

LOCAL ORGANISATION. 1,051 chemists nationwide, 134 opticians, 16 Childrens World stores, 8 photo centres and 1 beauty salon.

LOCAL GIVING. Special consideration is given to charities in the Company's area of operations, Nottingham in particular. Local managers can give small amounts of about £20 per charity, but this is not widely publicised since it is taken off each store's budget.

GIVING IN KIND. Gift vouchers of around £20 are also permitted. Some managers do give stock but gifts in kind are usually determined by head office. Collecting boxes are allowed, one to each floor. Branches are encouraged to support local charities. Some headquarters help is offered. For example, Boots is offering inner city school printing facilities for a school newspaper. There are also some training places offered to voluntary groups, on management development courses, report writing courses and public speaking.

STAFF ACTIVITIES. Boots does not in general second staff because it is considered that they get wide enough experience in their work in stores. There is no policy on staff volunteering but there is obviously time off for volunteering for public duties. There is a payroll giving scheme. Staff do collect widely for charity and last year raised £78,000. There is a policy of providing matching funds up to a certain amount. There are some very well organised staff charity committees at local level, for example, at the Boots Aldershot warehouse.

OTHER INFORMATION. Boots has fewer complaints now about the type of appeals received. Appeals are getting increasingly sophisticated. There has been a distinct reduction in number as a result of publicising Boots' policy, and appeals are better targetted. But far too much information is sent. Each appeal now needs more time and research on the part of Boots. Appeals to head office should go to Mrs P Dexter, Administrator, Boots Charitable Trust.

BRITANNIA BUILDING SOCIETY

Newton House
Leek
Staffs ST13 5RG   *Tel 0538 399149*

LOCAL ORGANISATION. 250 local branches throughout the country.

POLICY. In 1988 the Society and its subsidiary companies made charitable donations amounting to £4,572 (£2,810 in 1987). No contributions were made for political purposes. Because of the restrictions placed on building socities' charitable support, regrettably, charitable donations are small in amount. Each request is considered by a committee of directors.

LOCAL GIVING. So far as is practicable the Society makes donations to local charities in its main headquarters operation in North Staffordshire. This would include support for quasi-charitable events such as community arts festivals. National charities are in general not supported because if one appeal was accepted the Society would find it difficult to turn down other national appeals. Very exceptionally, branch managers can make donations of the order of £10-20. They have no donations budget and amounts would have to come from sponsorship and public relations. They can contribute to local charities by way, for example, of paying for Society advertising in a local charity journal.

STAFF ACTIVITIES. There is no explicit policy on involving staff in charitable support. The Society is pleased to give moral support where staff are involved, and to make the odd donation if the budget permits.

OTHER INFORMATION. Collecting boxes and other promotional devices for charities are not permitted in local branches because it is not possible to ensure fair coverage for all the different charities. Head office contact is Mr Roy Hughson, Secretary to the Society.

BRITISH AIRWAYS

Speedbird House
Heathrow Airport
Hounslow TW6 2JA   *Tel 081-759 5511*

POLICY. The company currently donates around £300,000 annually. It does not want to publicise its donations policies. It has annual charitable themes and staff-related charitable efforts.

LOCAL ORGANISATION. Represented at the major airports and some BA shops, BA is well known in the local areas where it has representation.

OTHER INFORMATION. The Company reports that it has more than enough requests and has no difficulty in making its donations. Head office contact is Jacqueline Cole, Charities Administrator.

BRITISH PETROLEUM PLC

Britannic House
Moor Lane
London EC2Y 9BU   *Tel 071-920 8000*

LOCAL ORGANISATION. Besides the many petrol sites across the country which are either operated directly by the Company or contracted to sell BP products, BP operates oil and refinery plants in the following locations (listed in descending order of number of employees): Grangemouth, Scotland; Hemel Hempstead, Hertfordshire; Llandarcy, South Wales; Aldridge, West Midlands; Aberdeen; and various small locations up and down the country (eg Jarrow where some 20 people are employed).

POLICY. One of the largest British companies with a very sizeable programme of support to the community. In 1988, BP was involved in the following (total amounts in brackets): educational relations (£1,900,000); community projects (£1,400,000); donations to charities (£2,400,000); arts sponsorship (£800,000); other sponsorships including Challenge to Youth (£500,000). £2 million was also donated to the Royal Society of Edinburgh for research in science and technology.

LOCAL GIVING. The Community Affairs Dept at head office has overall responsibility for the management of BP's support to charities and community groups, national and local. The major plants listed above will usually have their own public relations department with their own small operating budget for support to local charities. Consideration in these departments is also given to sponsorship programmes involving charities.

STAFF ACTIVITIES. Payroll giving and an extensive programme of secondment both operate in the Company. There is a matched giving scheme in which BP matches pound for pound up to a certain limit cash given to charities by staff. BP is currently considering matching time volunteered to charities by Company staff. Each major plant as well as head office has its own staff association with its own programme of involvement and support to charities.

OTHER INFORMATION. The contact at head office is Mr Gordon Smith, Manager, Community Affairs. Mr Chris Marsden is Manager, Educational Relations; Mr Robin Heal, Manager, Community

Projects; Mr Andrew Searle, Manager Donations; Mr Dudley Coates, Manager, Sponsorship; and Ms Sue Pesch, Sponsorship Manager, Public Relations Division, BP Oil, Hemel Hempstead (responsible for Challenge to Youth).

BRITISH RAIL

British Railways Board
Euston House
24 Eversholt St
PO Box 100
London NW1 1DZ   Tel 071-922 9276 *(for Community Unit)*

LOCAL ORGANISATION. Responsible for over 20,000 miles of lineside with over 2,400 stations. BR has a regional and area management structure.

POLICY. British Rail's 'Community Policy' is focussed in a special Community Unit at Rail headquarters. The policy is actioned through the local Regional and Business managers. BR does not give grants of a general nature but supports job creation, urban regeneration and environmental improvement. Policy is contained in four policy statements obtainable from the Community Unit. Artwork and environmental improvement on the railway are particularly stressed.

LOCAL GIVING. Area managers have only a certain amount of discretion to give to charities. Policy is set centrally and acted on regionally and locally.

GIVING IN KIND. BR cannot consider requests for such things as free rail travel.

STAFF ACTIVITIES. BR does second staff within the purposes of its Community Policy.

OTHER INFORMATION. Contact the Community Unit in the first instance.

BRITISH SHOE CORPORATION LTD

Sunningdale Rd
Leicester LE3 1UR   *Tel 0533 320202*

LOCAL ORGANISATION. Part of Sears PLC (see separate entry for Sears). Leicester-based head office for footwear manufacturing, warehousing and wholesaling. Operates chain of retail outlets trading as Freeman Hardy Willis, True Form, Curtess, Saxone, Bertie, Roland Cartier, Dolcis, Lilley and Skinner, Manfield, Shoe City. Also operates in Eire and the Netherlands. Sports retailing under the name of Olympus and SupaSports.

POLICY. In principle, requests for charitable donations are referred to the head office in Leicester.

LOCAL GIVING. Branches do not have authority to make donations. Local managers have some discretion over such things as poster display for charities and head office would not object to activities of this kind. With headquarters in Leicester, a good deal of support is given in this city and Leicestershire. The Company is heavily involved with a training centre in Leicester for the NSPCC and the Managing Director sits on the managing board for this. It also supports the Disabled Special Olympics and seconds a member of staff to assist with the organisation.

OTHER INFORMATION. The Company receives 'a fairly regular flow' of appeals. Most of them are fairly local though a few are more widely based. Head office contact is Mr S G Mountfield, Company Secretary.

BRITISH TELECOMMUNICATIONS PLC

81 Newgate St
London EC1A 7AJ   *Tel 071-356 5000*

POLICY. Charitable donations last year in excess of £2,300,000. There is a close relationship with such organisations as The Samaritans and Childline which make a lot of use of telephone services. There is an annual theme for charitable support. In 1989 it was new technology for elderly people.

LOCAL ORGANISATION. British Telecom is organised into 27 districts with a head office in each. Each head office has a charitable budget which is set centrally and which in 1989/90 amounted to £15,000 annually for each office. Offices can call on an additional like amount for special reasons.

LOCAL GIVING. Cash donations are left to local discretion, but generally if a donation amounts to more than £3,000 it is referred to headquarters. If more than £5,000, it goes to the Charity Committee at head office.

GIVING IN KIND. Donations of second-hand equipment, furniture and telephone apparatus such as answering machines are sometimes made. Free telephone services are not offered as this would be contrary to the licence under which the Company is permitted to provide telephone services.

STAFF ACTIVITIES. Staff are seconded to charitable and enterprise agencies, and policy on this is centrally controlled. A few staff are seconded locally. There is a policy of encouraging staff involvement in charities. There are awards for individual achievement, for groups of staff raising the most for charity and staff are sponsored for charitable events.

OTHER INFORMATION. The Company comments that of the charitable appeals it receives, some are good, others less than professional. All appeals should be accompanied by a set of accounts and if going to head office should be sent to Mrs C M Pecksen, .Community Affairs Dept.

BROOK STREET BUREAU
(See Blue Arrow PLC).

THE BURTON GROUP PLC
214 Oxford St
London W1N 9DF   *Tel 071-636 8040*

LOCAL ORGANISATION. Large fashion retailer with 1,600 outlets nationwide, through Burton, Topman, Principles, Dorothy Perkins, Topshop, Evans, Debenhams.

POLICY. Charitable donations last year of over £560,000. The Company is heavily involved in supporting enterprise agencies and a limited number of national charities.

LOCAL GIVING. Each division carries its own responsibility across the board, except charitable giving. No funds are available at local level for giving, either in cash or in kind. All giving has to have approval from head office. A policy of allowing local managers some discretion is now being considered, but this is difficult to implement with so many different divisions and shops. Head office reports that there is not much demand from the local level. Burton would support such things as a local hospital appeal or a national but localised disaster such as Hillsborough. With so many appeals, it is often 'a gut reaction' which decides where support should go.

STAFF ACTIVITIES. Staff are seconded, but not to local organisations. There is no policy on staff volunteering, though they are free to volunteer if they wish. There is a Give As You Earn scheme which attracts matched giving by the Company.

OTHER INFORMATION. The Company reports that the quality of charitable appeals received by head office varies a great deal. Nothing is considered without it being personally addressed and circular appeals are avoided. Appeals should be addressed to Mr Robin Carver, Group Charity Manager.

CHELTENHAM & GLOUCESTER BUILDING SOCIETY

Cheltenham House
Clarence St
Cheltenham
Gloucs GL50 3JR   *Tel 0242 236161*

LOCAL ORGANISATION. Buiding society branches across the country.

POLICY. Operates a small donations budget. Donations have recently gone to the Meningitis Trust, the Everyman Theatre in Cheltenham and the Gloucester Cathedral Fund.

LOCAL GIVING. Most support goes to charities in the region of head office. Managers are generally instructed to pass appeals to head office. They can do so with a recommendation if they wish.

OTHER INFORMATION. As with many building societies, charitable support is mainly attached to sponsorship programmes where the Society is under an obligation to get some return for its support. Further information is obtainable from Mr Gerry Angrave, Marketing Dept.

CHURCH AND CO PLC

St James
Northampton NN5 5BJ   *Tel 0604 51251*

LOCAL ORGANISATION. The Group is principally engaged in the manufacture, wholesale and retail distribution of footwear. It operates an extensive number of retail shops, trading as A Jones Plc, across the country and as Church and Co in Canada, the USA, Belgium and France.

POLICY. Donations to charitable organisations by the group in 1988 amounted to £5,025.

LOCAL GIVING. Locally directed appeals are in turn directed to head office. The Group has strong local connections with Northampton.

OTHER INFORMATION. Letters in the first instance should be addressed to Mr P A Hayward, Company Secretary, at head office.

C & J CLARK LTD

40 High St
Street
Somerset   *Tel 0458 43131*

LOCAL ORGANISATION. Besides nationwide shoe shops, the head office is in Somerset, the K Shoe factory in Kendal, Cumbria and the retail operation in Aldershot, Hants.

POLICY. The policy is quite clear. Giving is restricted to Somerset where the Company is based and where it considers that with relatively few commercial enterprises present in the county, local charitable support is all the more required. The Clark Foundation, a family trust, gives larger sums than the Company.

STAFF ACTIVITIES. Volunteering on the part of staff would be looked on favourably, but it is not encouraged in any special way. There is no policy on staff secondment to charities.

OTHER INFORMATION. The Company comments that about 50 appeals are received each week. Circular appeals are answered, but they are always turned down. Some appeals are accompanied by excessive amounts of literature. Head office contact is Mr Ian Ritchie, Public Relations Manager.

COMET GROUP PLC

George St
Hull HU1 3AU

Tel 0482 20681

LOCAL ORGANISATION. Part of Kingfisher Plc (see separate entry). Suppliers of electrical goods in over 300 nationwide outlets. Hull-based head office where the operation was founded some years ago.

POLICY. Kingfisher Plc allows Comet a separate charitable budget. Comet's policy generally is that rather than giving piecemeal to appeals received, the Company has a few regular subscriptions to a small number of charities that it wishes to support.

LOCAL GIVING. Charity appeals are generally not handled by local branches but dealt with by head office in Hull. Support to local charities is given by branches but is generally approved by head office. Since April 1989 the Company has been trying out a scheme of giving regional offices a small budget of some £5,000 per region for the year for donations to charities. The decisions are in the hands of Regional General Managers. The Company also tries to support some charities local to Hull, including a local hospice.

GIVING IN KIND. If donations local to branches are made, these are always in kind and normally are a small gift for a raffle prize etc or a small voucher. Gifts include audio and video material and small domestic appliances. Larger gifts such as TV's and video equipment might occasionally be obtainable from the Public Relations Dept at head office providing the appropriate public relations exercise can be found.

OTHER INFORMATION. General appeals to head office should be sent in the first instance to the Company Secretary's office.

COOPERATIVE BANK PLC

PO Box 101
1 Balloon St
Manchester M60 4EP   *Tel 061-832 3456*

LOCAL ORGANISATION. A wholly owned subsidiary of the Cooperative Wholesale Society (see separate entry). About 110 branches nationwide with main areas of strength in the North West and North East. Manchester and Skelmersdale have large administrative offices. There are also a number of branches in Greater London, Yorkshire and the Midlands. There are in addition 3,500 banking points in Cooperative Retail Societies.

POLICY. During 1988 the Bank made donations of £79,839 to UK charitable organisation. No donations were made for political purposes.

LOCAL GIVING. Approaches to local branches would invariably find their way to head office, although branch managers can always make recommendations. The Bank particularly favours charities local to its centre of operations. It is heavily involved, for example, in helping establish a Community Trust in Manchester in which money is raised locally and passed, usually in small amounts, to local charities.

STAFF ACTIVITIES. Staff local to Manchester are involved in the Community Trust. There are many local charities in which staff in the branches are involved. There is a payroll giving scheme and staff have been helping with support to Children in Need.

OTHER INFORMATION. The Bank comments that the central budget for donations could easily be spent ten times over. It is difficult to choose between the many deserving causes. Head office contact is through Mr David Smith (Public Relations) or Mr Rod Kilgour, Head of Marketing.

COOPERATIVE WHOLESALE SOCIETY

New Century House
Manchester M60 4ES   *Tel 061-834 1212*

LOCAL ORGANISATION. CWS is in the main composed of 85 local independent societies, each of which have a say in the running of the organisation. There are some retail outlets run directly from head office, in South East England, Scotland and Northern Ireland. There are also production centres and farms across the country.

POLICY. There is a central budget for donations to national charities. CWS continues to support the Woodcraft Folk for young people and is involved in job creation projects in inner city Manchester. There are no figures collated centrally on the amount of charitable giving.

LOCAL GIVING. The local picture varies a good deal. Each of the 85 local societies has its own policy on support to charities. Within the administrative operation serving the entire organisation, there are two trading divisions (retail and services, and production and property) and some 30 groups in both divisions. Each group within limits sets its own policy. Thus the milk group, with a number of factories and creameries across the country, might well support some charities local to its centres of operation. The local shops not controlled by the independent societies would refer appeals to the local regional office in London, Glasgow or Belfast. There is an expanding number of superstores which have their own small budget for charitable support.

STAFF ACTIVITIES. Staff in local stores are encouraged to take part in charitable events. There is a strong staff council in Manchester which supports local charities. There is also a staff payroll giving scheme.

OTHER INFORMATION. Head office contact through Mr Geoffrey Simpson, Corporate Affairs Dept.

CORAL RACING LTD

Glebe House
Vicarage Drive
Barking
Essex IG11 7NS   *Tel 081-591 5151*

LOCAL ORGANISATION. 1,008 betting shops across the country and one of Britain's largest chains. Part of Bass Group (see separate entry).

POLICY. Within the guidelines supplied by the parent company, Coral supports a number of charities from its own budget. The Company is closely involved, in view of its racing links, with the Spinal Injuries Association.

LOCAL GIVING. Branch managers and the 25 area managers generally do not have their own local budget for giving to charities and refer appeals to head office, but they do have some discretion to assist and can sometimes find ways of doing so from other budget heads. If a local manager telephoned with a recommendation, head office would try to do what it could.

OTHER INFORMATION. The Press Office or Public Relations Department have further information on charitable support.

COURAGE LTD

Ashby House
1 Bridge St
Staines
Middx TW18 4TP   *Tel 0784 466199*

LOCAL ORGANISATION. Large brewery operation with breweries in Reading, Tadcaster and Bristol in the UK and Cork in Ireland. Runs some 5,000 public houses across the country (the fifth largest brewery operation in the UK, measured by the number of pubs). Owned by the Australian group, Elders IXL.

POLICY. Courage has a charitable trust (the Courage Charitable Trust) which decides and distributes grants to charities. The policy tends to be 'to give a little to a lot', though there are some large annual donations made to a few charities. Donations are given 'across the board' to a large spread of charities and not just to those operating in a few particular fields. The smaller donations tend to be of the order of £25 to £50.

LOCAL GIVING. All donations are decided on from head office and any local operation of the Company would pass on requests to head office.

GIVING IN KIND. Cash donations are made by the Charitable Trust. Donations of Company products for raffles, tombolas etc are sometimes made by the operating plants, eg John Smith's Brewery, Tadcaster.

OTHER INFORMATION. All appeals for consideration by the Charitable Trust should go to Mr Ryan at head office or Mrs Patterson, his assistant.

COURTS (Furnishers) PLC

1 Central Rd
Morden
Surrey   *Tel 081-640 3322*

LOCAL ORGANISATION. 153 stores worldwide. 80 High St stores, mainly in Southern England and Wales, retailing household furniture, carpets, bedding, china and glass. Operates chain of out-of-town Mammoth Superstores. Substantial number of overseas stores, particularly in the West Indies, trading in a wide range of household products.

POLICY. Policy on giving is to provide modest donations, usually in the form of gift vouchers, if this is reasonably possible. Decisions are largely in the hands of a retired director of the company. Favoured areas are children, the elderly and health. Political organisations and bloodsport organisations are not donated to. Donations for charitable purposes in the UK amounted to £16,000 in 1989 (£11,000 in 1988).

LOCAL GIVING. All local managers are instructed to pass requests to head office.

STAFF ACTIVITIES. Staff are free to support charities, but there is no particular policy on charitable involvement.

OTHER INFORMATION. Head office comments that it receives many appeal letters. Two or three replies are sent each day on average. All requests go to Mr Todd, Assistant Company Secretary.

COVENTRY BUILDING SOCIETY

Economic House
PO Box 9
High St
Coventry CV1 5QN   *Tel 0203 555255*

LOCAL ORGANISATION. 65 branches, mainly in Coventry and the West Midlands.

POLICY. Charitable contributions of £1,066 in 1988. The Society tries to assist where it can but claims it is restricted in the amount of support it can give, 'as are all building societies'.

LOCAL GIVING. Charitable activities are particularly supported in the Coventry area.

STAFF ACTIVITIES. The Society's staff are actively involved in the Coventry area, currently on fund raising for a cancer ward for a local hospital. They are heavily involved in such things as fun runs and they are presently organising a Knock-A-Thon, knocking on local doors and collecting and counting the charitable donations.

OTHER INFORMATION. Local branches are able to help through sponsorship, providing there is some sort of business return to the Society. It may be a play or event of some description and the Society is able to donate prizes. At head office, contact may be made initially through the Secretary to the Society, Mr M H Ritchley.

CREST HOTELS

Bridge St
Banbury
Oxfordshire OX16 8RQ   Tel 0295 252555

LOCAL ORGANISATION. 49 hotels in the UK, 71 in the rest of Europe. Part of the Bass Group (see separate entry), although in the process of being sold off by the parent company.

POLICY. Head office deals with national charitable donations within the present guidelines laid down by Bass, the parent company.

LOCAL GIVNG. The company particularly supports charities in the Banbury area, the location of head office. Charities local to each hotel may also be supported. Appeals received by head office from charities local to hotels in the group are passed on to the relevant hotels in case they can provide support. Small cash donations are sometimes given.

GIVING IN KIND. Hotels and head office will occasionally help charities with the free provision of hotel accomodation.

STAFF ACTIVITIES. Local staff are actively involved with local charities. Staff quite often take part in such things as sponsored walks. There is no particular policy on encouraging involvement.

OTHER INFORMATION. The contact at head office is Mr David Sankey, Group Public Relations Manager.

CURRYS (See Dixons Group Plc.)

DIXONS GROUP PLC

29 Farm St
London W1X 7RD   *Tel 071-499 3494*

LOCAL ORGANISATION. High St retailers throughout the country of electrical and hi-fi goods. Trades as Dixons and Currys. Owns Supasnaps chain of 337 stores retailing cameras and accessories. Also recently acquired the 64 Wigfalls stores in the North and Midlands. At the time of going to press, the Company had received a take-over bid from Kingfisher Plc.

POLICY. Donations to registered charities in 1987-88 amounted to £248,000. The Group supports a carefully selected spectrum of needs covering welfare, education (including a proposed city technology college), arts and youth, but its particular interest is in inner city educational and training programmes. The donations list currently includes about 100 charities, including the Royal British Legion, Gt Ormond St Hospital, the Royal College of Physicians and the Malcolm Sargeant Appeal Fund for children with cancer.

LOCAL GIVING. Local branches have no budget for appeals. They cannot donate products, but they have some discretion to allow discounts of up to 20% on purchases by charities. All other appeals are passed to head office.

STAFF ACTIVITIES. There is a definite policy of encouraging stores to take part in such things as shopping precinct charitable events.

OTHER INFORMATION. The Company reports that it receives a considerable number of requests for help from charities. Head office contact initially should be made through Mr Richard Kalms, Director of Corporate Affairs.

ELECTRICITY COUNCIL

30 Millbank
London SW1P 4RD   *Tel 071-834 2333*

POLICY. Due to the forthcoming privatisation of the electricity supply industry, the Electricity Council expects to hand over certain responsibilitites to a new Electricity Association with effect from 1 January 1990. The Electricity Association will need to consider its position in relation to outside bodies such as charities, but it is too early at present to give any indication of this.

OTHER INFORMATION. Local Electricity Boards face similar reorganisation. Contact the Secretary's Dept at the above head office address (tel: ext 5272) or else your local Electricity Board.

ETAM PLC

Jubilee House
213 Oxford St
London W1R 2AH   *Tel 071-437 5655*

LOCAL ORGANISATION. Over 200 fashion retail outlets across the country, mainly trading as Etam and Tammy Girl. Acquired Snob and Peter Brown in 1987. Retailers mainly of female fashion.

POLICY. Many donations are made through a charitable fund handled by the Charities Aid Foundation. Contributions for 1988/89 amounted to £12,000 (up from £2,000 in 1987/88). All appeals are forwarded from branches to head office, whether they come from staff or from local charities. A management committee meets to decide on donations. Areas particularly favoured are women's organisations, since the company retails women's fashion, especially charities concerned with women's health. Cervical cancer, health in general, heart and children's organisations are examples of charities which normally benefit.

LOCAL GIVING. Not encouraged. All appeals are directed through head office.

STAFF ACTIVITIES. Local branches do get involved in local charities and in local fund raising, eg through such things as carnivals, but there is no particular Company policy on this.

OTHER INFORMATION. Head office contact is Mr Miles Drake, Company Secretary.

EXPRESS DAIRY

430 Victoria Rd
South Ruislip
Middlesex HA4 0HF　　　　　　　*Tel 081-842 5000*

LOCAL ORGANISATION. Milk and dairy products from plants nationwide to households in most regions. Part of Grand Metropolitan (see separate entry). Now trades as Grand Metropolitan Foods Europe.

POLICY. Overall guidelines are determined by the parent company. Express Dairy has its own small charitable budget.

LOCAL GIVING. Managers of local outlets are instructed to pass charitable requests to head office.

OTHER INFORMATION. The Legal Department at head office deals with support to charities.

FENWICK LTD

Elswick Court
Newcastle-upon-Tyne NE99 1AR　　　*Tel 091-232 5100*

LOCAL ORGANISATION. 8 department stores in the major cities.

POLICY. Charitable donations of nearly £40,000 last year. The Company is approached by many different charities and from many different branches within the same charity. Larger appeals are considered by head office. For example, if an approach was made by a local Red Cross branch then it would most probably be referred to head office.

LOCAL GIVING. Local managers have some discretion to give if a local approach is made and there is a small local charity budget at each local branch.

STAFF ACTIVITIES. There is no company policy here. There are no matched giving schemes run by the Company and no payroll giving schemes.

OTHER INFORMATION. The Company comments that head office often receives a myriad of different appeals from the same source. It may get as many as ten appeal letters, say, from ward sisters in the same hospital, and each has to be answered individually. Head office contact is Mr I J Dixon.

FORD MOTOR COMPANY LTD

Eagle Way
Brentwood
Essex CM13 3BW   *Tel 0277 253000*

POLICY. Much of Ford's charitable effort is channelled through the Ford of Britain Trust. The Ford Motor Co has an annual budget of some £2 million, but this is spent chiefly on secondment of pre-retirement staff and is not publicised by the PR Director. Appeals to the Company are normally passed to the Trust.

LOCAL ORGANISATION. The Company is represented in over twenty different locations in Britain, chiefly Dagenham (assembly), Bridgend (engines), Belfast (pump production), Basildon (tractors), Langley (trucks), Dunton, Essex (research and engineering). Ford car dealers are separately owned and independent of the Company.

LOCAL GIVING. The Trust is legally a separate entity from the

Company and its policy is independent of it, though trustees do recognise the responsibility the Company has to its factory locations. It has a policy of neighbourly help. There are no cash limits to its giving, though normally this is restricted to between £500 and £5,000. In practice, the bulk of the money goes to projects tackling deprivation, disability and social need.

GIVING IN KIND. The Trust cannot give in kind, but it is able, for example, to purchase minibuses from the Company for charitable purposes. The Company may be able to sponsor charities through giving minibuses.

STAFF ACTIVITIES. Many staff in the Company do get involved in fund raising, and there are secondment programmes to national charities. There are also payroll giving schemes, but the Trust is not empowered to match the giving here.

OTHER INFORMATION. The Trust comments that a large charity appeal might get rebuffed, only to be followed by an appeal from a local branch which is rebuffed in turn. The Trust feels that often there is insufficient head office-local branch liaison in charities. National charities need to rethink the purpose of arranging such things as royal receptions. An appeal letter of a few paragraphs is recommended, coming straight to the point. Appeals to the Trust should be addressed to the Trust Administrator, Mr John Kerr.

GATEWAY/ WOOLWICH EQUITABLE BUILDING SOCIETY

Corporate Headquarters
Watling St
Bexleyheath
Kent DA6 7RR   *Tel 081-854 2400*

LOCAL ORGANISATION. 550 branches across Britain.

POLICY. Charitable donations for the year ending September 1988 amounted to £103,000. The 'Community Services' budget is considerably larger, standing at around £450,000 at present, covering three corporate relations areas. Policy is changing. Until 1989 the Society gave in three areas: enterprise and the built environment; education, training and unemployment; and national charities. A revised scheme is to take effect in January 1990. The Society will continue to give to national charities as the appeals come into head office. It will also give to the arts. There will also be a 'community involvement programme' of giving to charities local to the Society's centres of operation. The subject areas for giving have yet to defined, but almost certainly educational programmes for youth and the older age groups will feature prominently.

LOCAL GIVING. The 'community involvement programme' is aimed at catchment areas local to head offices: Bexley, Greenwich, Lewisham, Bromley, North Kent and Worthing. Local charities in these areas will be able to apply for grants. Local charities outside these areas are able to apply to local branches but the finance available is very small. The Society has six regions with a charitable budget of only £2,000 per region.

OTHER COMMENTS. The stance of the Society to charities differs from the normal one of building societies. It does not consider that building societies are constrained constitutionally so far as supporting charities is concerned. Head office contact: Mr David Blake, Assistant General Manager, Corporate Affairs.

GATWICK AIRPORT LTD

Gatwick
West Sussex RH6 0NP   *Tel 0293 503096*

LOCAL ORGANISATION. Extensive airport operations in the Southern region. Part of BAA plc (see separate entry).

POLICY. A panel of managers currently decides cash allocation of £5,000 annually to charities. Usually, donations are made of between £100 and £200. Donations are normally made to whichever local charities write in asking for a donation, to charities in some way connected with members of staff and to charities which in some way will directly or indirectly benefit the operation of the airport. There is particular support given to a local hospice.

STAFF ACTIVITIES. Different staff sections and departments in the airport undertake fund raising exercises and support a range of charities.

OTHER INFORMATION. The contact is Mr David Hunt, Public Relations Manager.

GENERAL ACCIDENT FIRE AND LIFE ASSURANCE CORPORATION PLC

Pitheavlis
Perth
PH2 0NH   *Tel 0738 21202*

LOCAL ORGANISATION. Offices across the country, some with shop front exteriors, others behind the High St and on the outskirts of the main towns.

POLICY. The Board believes it has a duty to support not only charitable organisations, but the community at large, including the arts, education, science, and job creation. During 1988 the Corporation has been active in supporting these areas and in particular has made a further substantial commitment to the UK Road Safety Campaign. £257,534 was donated in 1988 to UK charitable organisations, mainly in the field of medical, aged and youth. An additional £1,341,000 went to 'other community involvement projects'. There was sponsorship of six university-based research projects in road user behaviour. £35,000 went to the Conservative Party.

LOCAL GIVING. The Corporation prefers to deal with the parent body of the local charity, if there is one. Local appeals do not stand much chance of funding, but there are always exceptions. Branch managers do have a little financial discretion depending on the size of the branch. Head office is located in Perth. Giving is not necessarily to Scottish charities since only some 10% of the insurance business comes from Scotland. General Accident operates a large overseas operation, but charitable support tends to be British-based.

OTHER INFORMATION. Appeals to head office should be directed to Mr A Cade, Company Secretary.

GRANADA GROUP PLC

36 Golden Square
London W1R 4AH   *Tel 071-734 8080*

LOCAL ORGANISATION. Mainly through the regional activity of Granada TV in the North West.

POLICY. Because of the large number of appeals the Group has to be fairly firm. A charity committee meets from time to time. Generally, giving is restricted to trade associations (cinema and TV) involving employees. There is a short list of national recipients such as the Royal Opera House.

LOCAL GIVING. Granada TV confines its giving to the North West and mostly to television-related areas. Subsidiary companies such as Granada TV Rental may be approached at High St level but giving is restricted to a very small scale.

STAFF ACTIVITIES. At Group level there is no special policy on volunteering or secondment. Payroll giving and secondment are under consideration by Granada TV.

OTHER INFORMATION. Head office comments that they are unable to fulfill many of the appeals received. Contact at head office for Granada Television is Ms K Arundale, Granada Television Ltd, TV Centre, Manchester M60 9EA.

GRAND METROPOLITAN PLC

11-12 Hanover Sq
London W1A 1DP   *Tel 071-629 7488*

LOCAL ORGANISATION. Besides breweries (Watney Mann and Truman) with some 1,500 pubs, Grand Metropolitan is represented at a local level by Express Dairies (see separate entry) and through its retail division by Berni Inn and Chef & Brewer (over 450 branded restaurants), hotels (1,400 rooms primarily in the UK), Peter Dominic (800 drinks retailing outlets) and Mecca Bookmakers and William Hill (1,700 betting offices).

POLICY. Contributions in 1988 of £512,000 to Grand Met Charitable Trust (£317,000 in 1987); £300,000 to Grand Met Community Services Trust (£245,000 in 1987); and £29,000 direct to individual charities (£22,000 in 1987). The Charitable Trust donated £281,000 (£241,000 in 1987) to non-trade related charities and £114,000 (£101,000 in 1979) to trade-related charities. In the US, Group companies donated £1,969,000.

About one third of Grand Metrolitan's charitable budget goes to trade-related charities (employees and ex-employees) and one third to three key areas settled on for the 1989-91 period: the British Sports Association for the Disabled, the Civic Trust and various inner-city projects and the National Asssociation of Boys Clubs. The remaining third goes to miscellaneous charities.

LOCAL GIVING. Managers at local level have discretion to give up to £50 only to any one appeal. Donations above this figure are steered through the central Grand Metropolitan Trust. Appeals are referred to head office with a recommendation from the local operating division. The trustees meet about quarterly to consider requests.

GIVING IN KIND. Express Dairies may give in kind to local events, through the provision of yoghurt and cream. The drinks division 'for obvious reasons' will not give away alchohol. The restaurants may give vouchers for meals.

STAFF ACTIVITIES. The local divisions of the Company can encourage such things as payroll giving schemes. Staff do collect for various charities. There is no scheme centrally to match what is done locally. The charity co-ordinator in each division is usually the Public Relations Director or Company Secretary. There is no charity committee at divisional level.

OTHER INFORMATION. The Company states that it receives many requests from charities and has to say 'no' to most. On the whole, the appeals are put together quite well. Applications to head office should go to Mr W T Halford, Group Public Affairs Director.

GREAT UNIVERSAL STORES PLC

251-256 Tottenham Ct Rd
London W1A 1BZ   *Tel 071-636 4080*

LOCAL ORGANISATION. The Company is only represented at local level through its Burberry stores division. Appeals there should be directed to the Managing Director.

POLICY. All giving is directed through the allied Wolfson Foundation.

OTHER INFORMATION. The head office contact is M Paschall, Senior Secretary.

GREENALL WHITLEY PLC

Wilderspool Brewery
Warrington WA4 6RH   *Tel 0925 51234*

LOCAL ORGANISATION. The seventh largest brewery chain with 1,626 public houses spread throughout the North West and

Midlands. Also owns Davenports Brewery, Birmingham, James Shipstone at the Star Brewery, Nottingham and the De Vere chain of hotels (30 in the UK including the Grand Hotel, Brighton and The Belfry, North Warwickshire).

POLICY. Charitable donations amounted in 1988 to £48,034. As a major employer in the North and Midlands, the Company is committed to help local and national initiatives in education, job creation and improving the environment. It has donated £49,000 to the Prince's Youth Business Trust (Greenall Whitley's Chairman chairs the £2 million North West Regional Appeal for this). It has also given three bursaries for business start-ups. A committee meets twice a year for dealing with large appeals.

LOCAL GIVING. The Company particularly favours links with the Warrington area, the North and Midlands generally. Local outlets of the Company are instructed to pass appeals to head office. Pub fundraising activities in 1988 were concentrated upon Children in Need, raising some £60,000.

OTHER INFORMATION. The contact for appeals at head office is through the Company Secretary's office.

GUARDIAN BUILDING SOCIETY

Guardian House
120 High Holborn
London WC1V 6RH   *Tel 071-242 3142*

LOCAL ORGANISATION. One of the few building societies without local branches. Guardian operates a borrowing operation from the head office.

POLICY. The Society donated some £2,000 in 1988. It makes a number of covenanted payments. Annually, the directors resolve to donate a certain amount according to requests received. The Society does not donate in any particular fields but looks at requests as they come in.

OTHER INFORMATION. Head office contact is Mr T E Howes, Secretary.

GUARDIAN ROYAL EXCHANGE PLC

Royal Exchange
London EC3V 3LS   *Tel 071-283 7101*

LOCAL ORGANISATION. Insurance branches across the country.

POLICY. In 1988 donations by the Group to charitable organisations amounted to £160,741. A contribution of £36,000 was paid to the British United Industrialists. In 1988 GRE suported enterprise schemes, community relations councils and the British Trust for Conservation Volunteers. Its Ipswich administrative office was involved in work experience schemes for disabled young people. Support was also given to crime and accident prevention. There were other charitable contributions, mainly in the field of medical and welfare national charities. Donations are made through a charitable trust. The Group does not favour giving to new charities, but to already established ones.

LOCAL GIVING. Local branches normally refer appeals to the Group's charitable trust. There is the occasional small donation made at local level, but nothing on a large scale. If an approach came from the local level to head office and if it merited further investigation, then the local administrative manager would be asked for a view on support. They are based at Ipwich, Lytham St Anne's, Edinburgh and London.

STAFF ACTIVITIES. There is a payroll giving scheme.

OTHER INFORMATION. Some 1500 appeals are received each year. There has been a recent tremendous increase in the number received. Numerous appeals fall outside the Group's guidelines. Appeals must be accompanied by a set of accounts. Loss-making charity events are not supported. Appeals to head office should be addressed to Ms A E Button, Appeals Secretary.

GUINNESS PLC

39 Portman Square
London W1 9HB   *Tel 071-486 0288*

LOCAL ORGANISATION. Represented locally through Glene-
agles Hotel, Scotland and Champney's health farm, Tring, Hertford-
shire, as well as breweries countrywide: United Distillers, Arthur
Bell (Scotland), Tanqueray Gordon, Arthur Guinness, Harp Lager,
Buckley's Brewery (England), together with breweries in Ireland,
Europe and Worldwide .

POLICY. In 1988 the Company made charitable contributions of
£498,000 (for the UK), £158,000 (for the Republic of Ireland) and
£69,000 (for overseas). Areas of benefit are particularly in education,
enterprise and youth. In the same year Guinness took a special
initiative with Relate (formerly the National Marriage Guidance
Council) and with the Cancer Research MacMillan Fund. It has
continued supporting the Dyslexia Educational Trust and has provided a Neurological Research Fellowship at The London Hospital.

LOCAL GIVING. The 'high powered' Donations Committee at
head office considers 99% of all appeals. Small donations of less than
£100 may be given locally.

STAFF ACTIVITIES. Includes secondment.

OTHER INFORMATION. Appeals to head office should be addressed to Mr J W Smart, Distillers House, 33 Ellersly Rd, Edinburgh
EH12 6JW.

HALIFAX BUILDING SOCIETY

Trinity Rd
Halifax
West Yorkshire HX1 2RG   *Tel 0422 365777*

LOCAL ORGANISATION. Operates one of the country's most
extensive chains of local building society branches.

POLICY. In the throes of reorganisation. The Society has recently established a community affairs department. In July 1989 a members' meeting sanctioned giving to charities in the areas of homelessness, job creation (with special emphasis on youth), the elderly and handicapped, and special medical research. For the present, environmental voluntary groups are ruled out. There is an undisclosed target budget for donations for the period ending January 1990, and the annual budget for the period following is up for review.

LOCAL GIVING. There is no local or regional budget, and the setting up of the community affairs department means that local budgets are unlikely for the immediate future. But appeals from local charities in the region of Calderdale, where the Society has a large administrative base, would be favourably regarded. The Society is a major participant in the Business in the Community demonstration project for the revitalisation of Halifax.

OTHER INFORMATION. Head office contact is Mr Jim Murgatroyd, Public Affairs Officer.

HEATHROW AIRPORT LTD

Hounslow
Middlesex   *Tel 081-748 4108*

LOCAL ORGANISATION. The UK's largest airport with extensive operations to the west of London. Part of BAA plc (see separate entry).

POLICY. Ad hoc grants currently up to £500 are made to some charities local to the airport. The local branch of the St John Ambulance is supported and a covenant goes to Heathrow Travel Care (an airport-based social work agency). Heathrow also has collecting boxes placed around the airport terminals and the central area for the collection of unwanted foreign exchange. Until recently some seven national charities benefitted fron the collection. But as from April 1989 it was decided that five local charities and the Gt Ormond St Hospital appeal would be the beneficiaries.

OTHER INFORMATION. Mr Garry May, Public Relations Manager, is the contact.

HOUSE OF FRASER PLC

1 Horwick Place
London SW1P 1BH   *Tel 071-834 1515*

LOCAL ORGANISATION. More than 70 High St stores, trading under different names. Besides the flagship store of Harrods in Knightsbridge, London, there is Dingles in the West, Howells in Wales and Binns in the North.

POLICY. Charitable donations last year in excess of £150,000. There is no set policy. Primarily the Board is responsible to its shareholders, though 'there is the recognition that the Company has an element of responsibility to voluntary organisations'. Each appeal is considered on its merits. There is no set amount that is donated, though 'no more than is appropriate' is given. There are certain undisclosed charities to which the Company covenants. Appeals from the local level would not be excluded from consideration by head office. There is no company charitable trust.

LOCAL GIVING. All appeals are sent to head office as a matter of policy. There is no local budget for dealing with appeals.

GIVING IN KIND. Store managers may give the odd £25 or £50 gift voucher.

STAFF ACTIVITIES. There is no specific policy on staff volunteering. There is no secondment of staff to charities.

OTHER INFORMATION. The Company comments that it is inundated with circular letters from charities. If charities do write in, they should take the trouble of addressing a personal letter. Appeals should be addressed to Mr J R P Davies, Company Secretary.

ICELAND BEJAM

1 Garland Rd
Honeypot Lane
Stanmore
Middlesex HA7 1LE   *Tel 081-951 3366*

LOCAL ORGANISATION. 450 stores nationwide including Scotland and Wales.

POLICY. An attempt is made to help on a small scale at local level.

LOCAL GIVING. All store managers pass requests to the Stanmore office PR Dept. About 200 letters are received each month and approximately £1,000 is given per month, often in kind. Where stores are located in shopping centres, then a little bit more is usually given if needs be, to match the giving of other neighbouring stores.

GIVING IN KIND. Often gifts are in kind, in terms of raffle prizes and food vouchers. Requests for equipment cannot usually be met, though the Stanmore office sometimes gives out cookery books and T-shirts for fun runs.

STAFF ACTIVITIES. There is fund raising by staff. For instance, the staff social club nationwide recently raised £10,000 for Guide Dogs for the Blind. Staff in all stores are encouraged to take part in fund raising. There is no secondment of staff.

OTHER INFORMATION. The Stanmore office contact is Mrs V Joseph, Public Relations Dept.

JOHN LEWIS PARTNERSHIP PLC

4 Old Cavendish St
London W1A 1EX   *Tel 071-637 3434*

LOCAL ORGANISATION. 21 department stores across the country trading under various names such as John Lewis, Peter Jones, Jones Bros, Pratts, Heelas, Tyrell and Green, Knight and Lee, Caleys, Trewin Bros, Jessop and Son, Robert Sayle, Bonds, Cole Bros, George Henry Lee and Bainbridge. 83 Waitrose supermarkets concentrated in the South of England.

POLICY. Charitable donations were made in 1988 amounting to £651,000. The Chairman and management of the Partnership normally deal with appeals for the arts and learning. The staff Central Committee for Claims which deals with national appeals donates to medical research, care of the elderly, children and youth, the mentally and physically handicapped, conservation and wildlife, and some money is reserved for disaster appeals.

LOCAL GIVING. Policy on giving is not written down, but there are guidelines to ensure standardisation of giving across the branches. Religious and political appeals are not met. The amount of each donation is not limited but branches must not spend over their total allocation. The total estimate that each staff committee has to work to is given at the beginning of the year –the estimate varies according to the size of the branch–and then running estimates are calculated by each committee.

GIVING IN KIND. Giving is in cash and in kind. There are many requests for such things as raffle prizes.

STAFF ACTIVITIES. Staff in each store elect a Committee for Claims which looks at all local appeals. The Waitrose supermarkets all elect one committee in their headquarters in Bracknell, Berkshire. Staff give a lot of charitable support. Sponsorships are not permitted and direct donations are given. There is no staff secondment.

OTHER INFORMATION. The Central Committee for Claims which deals with national appeals reports that it is irritating to receive multiple copies of the same letter from different branches of a charity..

Applications to head office should be addressed to the Central Committee for Claims, Medway House, 12-14 Clipstone St, London W1A 3AY.

JOHN MENZIES PLC

Hanover Buildings
Rose St
Edinburgh EH2 2YQ   *Tel 031-225 8555*

LOCAL ORGANISATION. 310 Menzies shops across the country, 150 Early Learning Centres and Hammicks book stores in the South.

POLICY. In 1988 the Company made charitable contributions of £55,000. There is no formal policy. A charity committee meets from time to time to review giving. Giving tends to be concentrated in Edinburgh and Scotland.

LOCAL GIVING. There is some local giving in Scotland, eg to the Lothian Association of Boys' Clubs. All appeals to local branches are passed to head office.

GIVING IN KIND. There is some giving in kind, but this is controlled from head office.

STAFF ACTIVITIES. Where staff volunteer, they are supported by the Company.

OTHER INFORMATION. Appeals should be directed to the Company Secretary at head office.

JOSHUA TETLEY & SON LTD

PO Box 142
The Brewery
Leeds LS1 1QG   Tel 0532 435282

LOCAL ORGANISATION. The Company operates a string of public houses in Yorkshire and the Midlands, and a brewery operation in Leeds. Parent company is Allied Lyons (see separate entry).

POLICY. Besides directing sizeable appeals to the head office of the parent company, Joshua Tetley has a small charitable budget of its own. Cash giving is usually divided up into 'very small donations' to particular charities. A wide range of charities is supported.

LOCAL GIVING. The Company tends to favour charities in its geographical area of operations.

GIVING IN KIND. The Company has been known to give office furniture and computers it no longer needs. It also donates Company products for raffle purposes.

STAFF. Policy on staff involvement in charitable work is presently rather 'fragmented and haphazard'. The Company believes in supporting the community and is trying to give more direction to policy. Secondment to charities is carried out and two members of staff in the company are seconded at the moment, including to the Churches' Urban Fund.

OTHER COMMENTS. The Company at present is in the process of defining more clearly which community groups and charities it will support. Currently three is a feeling that it is supporting perhaps too wide a range. Head office contact is Mr Graham Kershaw, Company Secretary.

KINGFISHER PLC

North West House
119 Marylebone Rd
London NW1 5PX

Tel 071-724 7749

LOCAL ORGANISATION. The parent company of operating companies with nationwide outlets, Woolworths, Superdrug, B & Q, Comet (see separate entries).

POLICY. In 1988-89 Kingfisher's estimate of its contributions to community projects was £611,000. This included payments for charitable purposes of £361,000. The rest was made up of donations in kind and the value of secondments. A further £1.8 million was raised for Comic Relief through the sale of red noses in Woolworth stores. The Company runs an extensive 'community involvement' programme. Target charities for 1988-89 have been NSPCC (Comet), NCH (Superdrug and Woolworths), Barnardo's (Charlie Browns Auto-centres), The Prince's Youth Business Trust and Children in Need (B & Q) and Help a Child to See (Woolworths). Crime prevention, enterprise initiative, women's issues and homelessness have also been favoured areas. Kingfisher does not generally support appeals which are exclusive to local projects or individuals, or which are largely for the restoration of building fabric.

LOCAL GIVING. Effectively, the operating companies have small budgets to meet requests for local appeals.

GIVING IN KIND. 'Giving in cash could get out of hand when you are talking about 800 stores' so giving in kind is much more the norm, for such things as raffle prizes. Each operating company varies in how they respond to appeals. Giving of products rather than cash is favoured. The operating companies tend to adopt different charities. For example, Comet is currently supporting the NSPCC.

STAFF ACTIVITIES. Employees get involved in a great deal of fund raising. In 1988-89 they raised over £275,000.

OTHER INFORMATION. Collecting boxes are not particularly favoured, especially in stores with check-outs where delays can cause problems. The head office contact Mr Tim Clement Jones, Company Secretary.

KWIK-SAVE GROUP PLC

Warren Drive
Prestatyn
Clwyd LL19 7HU   **Tel 07456 87111**

LOCAL ORGANISATION. 575 locations in England and Wales, principally as small 'no nonsense' foodstores under the Kwik-Save name. Also 22 Lateshopper shops in Lincolnshire, Humberside and South Yorkshire.

POLICY. The charitable contributions of the company amounted to £2,350 in 1988 (£2,146 in 1987). All appeals are steered to PR, Sales and Marketing at head office. Some 200 appeals are received each week and they are becoming 'an administrative headache'. The Company is about to adopt one charity -the Chest, Heart and Stroke Association- in order to concentrate its charitable support and hopefully cut down on the number of appeals. Support for this one charity will be publicised amongst staff, though this does not mean to the exclusion of all other charities.

LOCAL GIVING. Charitable appeals to local managers are normally redirected to head office.

GIVING IN KIND. Local managers may give the occasional product for local raffles etc in aid of charity.

STAFF ACTIVITIES. Head office wants to encourage staff to be involved. The Company is sizeable but it has 'a lean staffing structure' and there is no secondment of staff.

OTHER INFORMATION. Appeals in the first instance should go to the office of the Managing Director, Mr Graeme Seabrook.

LAURA ASHLEY HOLDINGS PLC

Carno
Powys SY17 5LQ   *Tel 0686 24050*

LOCAL ORGANISATION. Shops nationwide (164) and international (275), with headquarters and manufacturing in Wales as well as a distribution centre in Milton Keynes.

POLICY. Giving takes place with national and local charities. Donations for charitable purposes in the UK amounted in 1988 to £144,465. A charity committee of 5 or 6 people meets every two months to make decisions. Giving can be to local hospitals and hospices, for example, particularly at Christmas time. The Company has established its own charitable trust and three directors of the Company are trustees.

LOCAL GIVING. The Company likes to give in areas where there is a substantial company presence, in Wales for example. There is giving locally where there are shops and local managers are approached, but all requests to local stores are passed to head office. There is a separate charitable budget. Donations have ranged up to £5,000, but generally they are of the order of £25-50.

GIVING IN KIND. There is no giving in kind.

OTHER INFORMATION. The Company reports that 'many, many letters are received'. 130 is a typical number to go before each meeting of the Charities Committee. Decisions are made according to each request. Money goes to 'needy causes' and at Christmas time to the major charities. The Company contact is Mr Idwal Evans, Charity Coordinator.

LEEDS AND HOLBECK BUILDING SOCIETY

105 Albion St
Leeds LS1 5AS   *Tel 0532 459511*

LOCAL ORGANISATION. 73 branches across the country.

POLICY. The Society does support a number of charities. But its rules state that support has to be by way of a business arrangement. It is not permitted simply to donate to charities.

LOCAL GIVING. The Society supports charities across the country, but it has a particular presence in the Yorkshire region and would look especially favourably on charities there. All support goes in the form of sponsoring advertising for charities, paying for charity brochures, taking up advertising for fund raising events and the like. Approaches to local branches would normally be referred to head office.

OTHER INFORMATION. The contact at head office is Mr J Nuttal, Assistant General Manager.

LEEDS PERMANENT BUILDING SOCIETY

Permanent House
The Headrow
Leeds LS1 1NS   *Tel 0532 438181*

LOCAL ORGANISATION. 482 building society branches and 119 estate agencies across the country.

POLICY. During 1988 charitable donations amounted to £15,384. There is a central budget allocation for charities. Leeds Permanent was one of the forerunners in participating in a Visa affinity card scheme whereby for every £100 spent by the customer, 10p goes to certain charities (Imperial Cancer, Mencap, British Heart Foundation). 'Quite a lot of donations' go to charities through this route. Each appeal is considered on its merits. The Public Relations Manager sees all appeals. Decisions are necessarily subjective, and support through the Visa card system avoids the need for difficult decisions. The figure for the total amount donated is obscured by the fact that some support is offered through sponsorship schemes, and straight donations are not accounted for separately.

LOCAL GIVING. Support for charities, local and national, normally is channelled through the Corporate Communications Dept at head office unless the local branch sees fit to do something on a small scale. Head office has recently reorganised the whole accounting system and introduced local cost centres. This will make it possible to trace local giving better. Local managers do not have a special budget for charitable supports but would support and sponsor 'for good business reasons'.

OTHER INFORMATION. Head office contact is Wendy Kellingham, Publis Relations Manager.

LEGAL AND GENERAL GROUP PLC

Temple Court
11 Queen Victoria St
London EC4N 4TP   *Tel 071-248 9678*

LOCAL ORGANISATION. Insurance offices nationwide.

POLICY. During 1988 donations totalling £156,300 were made for charitable purposes. £25,000 was donated to the Conservative Party. Legal and General has an extensive community affairs policy, annually reviewed by the Group Board. Includes support to 14 enterprise agencies, a range of schools projects and arts sponsorship. Small covenanted payments to charities are being replaced by larger, single donations with involvement of Group staff. The Group does not give to sport for the able-bodied, to individuals, nor does it sponsor advertising.

LOCAL GIVING. A proportion of funds is set aside for small donations and Community Affairs staff do try to visit requesting charities to evaluate requests. Local managers can use their own budget for charitable support but normally they pass requests to head office. The help given is usually small and 'one-off' in order to enlarge the number of organisations helped.

GIVING IN KIND. Legal and General do give in kind for raffle prizes and other fund raising events. Their umbrellas, which feature in their advertising, are particularly in demand as items for raffles.

STAFF ACTIVITIES. Staff engage in a wide variety of fund raising activities. Legal and General are discussing whether this activity could be focussed on a few charities.

OTHER INFORMATION. As many as 2,000 requests each year are received by the Community Affairs Dept, of which about 80 were supported last year. A brochure from the Department is in preparation. Requests should initially go to the Community Affairs Department.

LIBERTY PLC

210-220 Regent St
London W1R 6AH   *Tel 071-734 1234*

LOCAL ORGANISATION. 22 branches of furnishing outlets nationwide.

POLICY. Charitable donations in 1988 of £3,574. Covenants are made to trade charities, mainly the textile benevolent funds, and to cottage homes in the textile trade. Local managers will pass all appeal letters to head office if they feel they should receive consideration.

LOCAL GIVING. The Company does not normally give in cash to local charities.

GIVING IN KIND. All local giving is in kind, never in cash. This might be in the form of fabric for volunteers to make up for charitable purposes, or it might be such things as silk scarves for use as raffle prizes.

STAFF ACTIVITIES. Staff involvement in charities is simply left to the discretion of staff.

COMMENTS ON APPEALS. Head office reports that it is inundated with appeals, but each one is treated individually on its merits. The head office contact is Miss Rita Howell in the Chairman's office.

THE LITTLEWOODS ORGANISATION

100-110 Old Hall St
Liverpool L70 1AB

Tel 051-235 2222

LOCAL ORGANISATION. A large trading and retail organisation, with a pools division, mail order business and credit and data marketing services. Represented locally through its chain store division of 113 chain stores nationwide.

POLICY. In 1988 the Company made charitable donations amounting to £67,711. In addition the Company makes large donations to the Football Trust. £10,000 has also been given to the National Association of Boys' Clubs. The Company is also closely associated with the John Moores Foundation.

LOCAL GIVING. Store managers do make small donations at the local level. Giving is pretty limited and much is controlled from head office.

GIVING IN KIND. All giving is in cash, never in kind.

STAFF ACTIVITIES. The Company operates the WorkAid payroll giving agency. No staff are seconded. There is no policy on giving time off for staff to volunteer – it is left to local discretion.

COMMENTS ON APPEALS. The Company reports that it is 'inundated' with appeals but otherwise has no comment to make. Head office contact is Mr J Wilkinson, Company Secretary.

LO-COST STORES
(See Argyll Group PLC.)

LLOYDS BANK PLC
Corporate Communications
PO Box 178
Antholin House
71 Queen St
London EC4N 1SL   *Tel 071-329 0798*

LOCAL ORGANISATION. One of the big four banks with branches nationwide.

POLICY. Currently some £1 million goes in contributions to charities, three-quarters of the money going to charities in the UK. The policy is generally to spread contributions as widely as possible in order to reflect shareholders' diverse interests and views on support to the community. Donations can be classified under five headings: care of the sick and disadvantaged, advancement of medicine, restoration and protection of heritage, education and research and support to the arts. The Bank also operates an extensive sponsorship programme, as well as giving support to inner city and employment programmes.

LOCAL GIVING. About one quarter of the total amount donated is allocated regionally. The regional structure is in the process of being changed and a new structure should be in place by 1990. Some regional offices decide to allocate so much to each branch while others deal according to changing demand. Where local branch managers have to deal with regional allocations, they are expected to put forward recommendations. Donations are only made to local charities which purely meet a local need, and appeals from these sources received by head office are passed to the relevant regional office.

GIVING IN KIND. The bank has little equipment free to donate. Many bank managers act as treasurers to local voluntary groups and often house the accounts in the bank.

STAFF ACTIVITIES. Fund raising support from staff to charities is matched by the Bank pound for pound, up to a pre-set level. Over 200 schemes annually are matched. There is also a Give-As-you-Earn scheme. Staff are involved closely with local charities, often acting as organisers and treasurers.

OTHER INFORMATION. Head office contact should be made through the Corporate Communications Dept.

Wm LOW & CO PLC

Baird Avenue
Dryburgh Industrial Estate
Dundee
DD1 9NF   *Tel 0382 814022*

LOCAL ORGANISATION. 63 supermarkets and freezer centres in Scotland and Northern England.

POLICY. Total charitable donations were limited last year to £7-10,000. There is no fixed policy. Small donations are determined by the Finance Director, Mr H L Findlay. Larger donations are handled by three directors.

LOCAL GIVING. Donations are not normally given to national appeals. More consideration is given to appeals based in Scotland. Appeals are generally passed to head office. Local managers can exercise very little discretion in giving.

GIVING IN KIND. Local managers may occasionally give products for such things as raffles.

OTHER INFORMATION. Head office reports that it receives several appeals each day and cannot deal with them all. What is dealt with depends on the type of application: 'The less personal letter and circulars obviously do not get the same amount of consideration as personally addressed appeals'. The head office contact is Mr H L Findlay, Finance Director.

MFI FURNITURE GROUP LTD

Southon House
333 The Hyde
Edgware Rd
London NW9 6TD   Tel 081-200 8000

LOCAL ORGANISATION. 164 branches UK-wide of furniture retailers and manufacturers. Also has acquired Schreiber kitchens (along with some High St outlets) and Hygena.

POLICY. Donations to charitable organisations amounted to £94,000 in the year ending 29 April 1989 (£45,000 in the previous year). Current emphasis given to supporting National Children's Homes, following survey of staff regarding charitable support. For the last three years resources have been largely directed at NCH. This has included placing collecting boxes for the NCH on branch premises and sponsoring NCH events. All appeal letters are replied to, but as a general rule the answer would be in the negative.

LOCAL GIVING. Some charities local to head office in Colindale are supported, particularly at Christmas time. Branches will consider local appeals and consideration will also be given at head office to requests from staff for support to particular charities.

STAFF ACTIVITIES. Often directed at supporting NCH through events like inter-store charity football.

OTHER INFORMATION. Contact at head office though the Chairman, Mr D S Hunt, or Secretary, Mr J D Randall.

McDONALD'S HAMBURGERS LTD

11-59 High Rd
East Finchley
London N2 8AW   *Tel 081-883 6400*

LOCAL ORGANISATION. A nationwide chain of 306 fast food restaurants mostly directly owned by the Company and very few of which are franchised.

POLICY. Charitable donations in 1988 of £26,459. Giving is very much on a small basis and business-related, and often co-ordinated through the PR Dept at head office.

LOCAL GIVING. Sometimes the local store will deal with a small appeal or telephone the PR Dept for advice. Links with charities are usually on the basis of making support a 'fun event'. For instance, the PR Dept handles the bookings for Ronald McDonald the clown to appear at charity events. Demand is heavy and bookings are made one year in advance. The PR Dept also arranges for the loan of orange drinks machines, for which a small charge is made. Meal vouchers can also be given as charity prizes and local stores sometimes sponsor Company advertisements in local charity magazines.

OTHER INFORMATION. Contact the Public Relations Dept in the first instance.

MARKS & SPENCER PLC

Michael House
37-67 Baker St
London W1A 1DN   *Tel 071-935 4422*

LOCAL ORGANISATION. Major countrywide retailers of clothing, furnishings and food.

POLICY. A major corporate giver with a community policy budget amounting to some £4.3 million in 1987/88. This includes giving from the Community Affairs Dept at head office in the fields of community welfare, medical, arts, and enterprise agencies, as well as the costs of secondments and participation in the Youth Training Scheme.

LOCAL GIVING. Local support from stores amounted in 1987/88 to some £220,000. Branches are allocated an annual budget for cash giving and a committee involving staff usually meets monthly to decide allocations. Giving is often to local charities.

GIVING IN KIND. Amounted to £200,000 in 1987/88. This is often in the form of gift vouchers. Food items are sometimes available towards the end of their shelf life.

OTHER INFORMATION. Each branch receives 'quite a lot of letters', including many for such things as school fêtes. Collecting boxes are not accepted for placing in stores. The head office contact is Mrs H T Allery, Manager, Community Affairs.

MIDLAND GROUP
Poultry
London EC2P 2BX   *Tel 071-260 8000*

LOCAL ORGANISATION. Banking and financial services with some 1,500 bank branches in the UK.

POLICY. The Group donated just under £700,000 to charities in 1988. Support to the voluntary sector covers welfare, care in the community, work and unemployment and inner city rejuvenation. Generally, education, support to overseas organisations and 'bricks and mortar' projects are excluded.

LOCAL GIVING. A small sum of the overall total is allocated to regions for giving locally, on the recommendation of local bank managers and according to internal policy guidelines laid down by the Board. Local appeals sometimes turn up at head office and these are usually passed to the relevant region. The Group separately considers local sponsorship events, where, say, a school or local brass band is seeking support and there could be a publicity return to the Group.

STAFF ACTIVITIES. There are two 'very extensive and expensive' schemes organised by the Group. One is a matching scheme where the Group gives £1 for every £1 raised by an employee, up to a maximum of £50. (Where time is contributed to a voluntary organisation, this is calculated at £5 per hour and matched). The other scheme involves payroll giving, and a matching contribution by the Group of up to £50.

OTHER INFORMATION. Appeals directed to head office should go initially to Mr A Furniss, Group Corporate Affairs, Public Relations.

Wm MORRISON SUPERMARKETS LTD

Hilmore House
Thornton Rd
Bradford BD8 9AX   *Tel 0274 494166*

LOCAL ORGANISATION. 44 stores across Yorkshire, Lancashire and as far north as Carlisle and south to Newark and Stamford.

POLICY. £115,000 in charitable donations in 1988. Giving is mostly handled at head office, but the Company does not want to disclose policy.

LOCAL GIVING. Local managers can give in cash and in kind to a very small degree.

OTHER INFORMATION. Head office contact is Mr M Ackroyd, Company Scretary.

NFC PLC

The Merton Centre
45 St Peters St
Bedford MK40 2UB   *Tel 0234 272222*

LOCAL ORGANISATION. Formerly known as the National Freight Consortium, the Company is mainly represented in the High St through Pickfords Travel, one of the largest U.K. retail travel agencies.

POLICY. The Social Responsibilities Council of the Company gave £237,000 in 1988. This sum includes responsibility for developing a visitors' service for retired employees and social activities for the Company's Pensioners' Association.

LOCAL GIVING. Most requests to local branches of Pickfords are passed to head office. They are sorted into categories and a central committee meets quarterly to decide on allocations.

GIVING IN KIND. There is no giving in kind.

OTHER INFORMATION. Pickford's High St branches will normally pass appeals to head office. But they may occasionally decide for sponsorship and publicity reasons to back an appeal by, for example, the offer of a free holiday for a raffle. The cost of this would be deducted from Pickford's publicity budget. The head office contact for charities is Mrs S Holderness.

NATIONAL AND PROVINCIAL BUILDING SOCIETY

Provincial House
Bradford
West Yorkshire BD1 1NL   *Tel 0274 733444*

LOCAL ORGANISATION. 327 branches nationwide, including Scotland, with a concentration of branches in Yorkshire.

POLICY. During 1988 the Society made contributions to charitable organisations amounting to £28,000. There is particular support for the National Children's Home.

LOCAL GIVING. No firm information, but it is understood that the Society particularly favours charities with a Yorkshire connection.

OTHER INFORMATION. Head office contact is Rita Donaghue, Public Relations.

NATIONAL WESTMINSTER BANK PLC

41 Lothbury
London EC2P 2BP   *Tel 071-726 1000*

LOCAL ORGANISATION. The largest of the big four banks in the UK with the largest number of branches countrywide.

POLICY. As with all the big four banks, Nat West has an extensive community support programme. The bank reports total community contributions of £9.7 million and charitable donations of £1.65 million. The overall budget includes support to national and local organisations, but these figures are not broken down for publication.

LOCAL GIVING. A 'certain sum' is allocated annually to regional offices for giving to local charities. Local branch managers do not have direct control over donations to local charities, but they are free to make recommendations. Requests are sent to regional office and the decisions are finally made there. Regional offices are given internal guidelines to follow, and these vary from year to year. Generally speaking, regional offices would steer clear of giving to local charities if head office was making a donation to the national office of the same charities.

GIVING IN KIND. There is 'not a tremendous amount of giving in kind'. But on occasions items can be found for fund raising events, eg T-shirts, pens with Nat West emblems.

STAFF ACTIVITIES. Staff are heavily involved with charities at the local level, but there is no set policy of asking staff to become involved. The line taken is that staff must feel free to make their own decisions on involvement, so that career prospects are not affected one way or the other. Voluntary organisations involving Bank staff are entitled to apply to the Bank for donations. The Bank also operates a matched giving scheme, matching the contributions of employees to charities up to a certain limit.

OTHER INFORMATION. The Sponsorship and Community Affairs Dept is the channel at head office through which appeals are made.

NATIONWIDE ANGLIA BUILDING SOCIETY

Chesterfield House
Bloomsbury Way
London WC1V 6PW　　　　　　　　*Tel 071-242 8822*

LOCAL ORGANISATION. An extensive network thoughout the UK of building society branches (870) and estate agents (470).

POLICY. The Society made charitable donations in the year ending 4 April 1989 amounting to £158,000. No contributions were made for political purposes.

LOCAL GIVING. The budgeting for charities is not divided between local and national charities. Some giving is national, some local. The Society has large administrative offices in Northampton and Swindon, and there is a small budget for donations to local charities in these two towns. If a local charity were to approach a local branch, the branch manager would probably refer to the regional office. The regional manager (there are more than 40 across the UK) has a limited budget to support local charity and community events in order 'to promote goodwill'. There is a certain amount of discretion at local level. Some branch managers have been known to turn down flat a local appeal. Some regional managers have been known to distribute their local budget for charitable support automatically to branch managers. There is no explicit written policy.

STAFF ACTIVITIES. At a local level, this varies. Staff are often heavily involved in fund raising events such as sponsored walks, bed pushes and the like. There is a Give As You Earn scheme, and the Society is about to give a special promotion to charitable donations made by staff.

OTHER INFORMATION. At head office, sponsorship is dealt with by Mr Nigel Snell, Public Relations Dept. Donations are handled by Mr V J Marsh, Nationwide Anglia, Moulton Park, Northampton NN3 1NL.

NEXT PLC

Desford Rd
Enderby
Leicester LE9 5AT   *Tel 0533 866411*

LOCAL ORGANISATION. Besides the nationwide chain of stores, Next has its headquarters in Leicestershire and some giving is concentrated here.

POLICY. A charities committee deals with large, often national, donations. The Leicester Royal Infirmary and the Special Olympics are currently examples of recipients of large donations. Head office receives an average of 7 letters per day. Appeals must be made in writing and if they are worthwhile, then sometimes a gift can be made.

LOCAL GIVING. Small, local giving directed at stores is handled centrally through the Executive office at headquarters.

GIVING IN KIND. The most common form of small, local giving is through the gift of vouchers and small products for raffle prizes, etc. Local stores are not empowered to give.

OTHER INFORMATION. Appeals to head office should be directed to the Chairman's office.

NORTHERN ROCK BUILDING SOCIETY

Northern Rock House
Gosforth
Newcastle upon Tyne NE3 4PL   *Tel 091-285 7191*

LOCAL ORGANISATION. 120 branches across Britain from Inverness to Brighton, with a concentration in the North East.

POLICY. A central charitable fund is administered by the directors.

LOCAL GIVING. The Society favours applications from charities in the North East and has helped charities here 'in all fields of work'. Each of its three local boards, in Manchester, London and Edinburgh, has a very small budget for charitable support. Local appeal letters would normally go to head office if a local branch manager wanted to make a recommendation.

STAFF ACTIVITIES. There is a payroll giving scheme in operation.

OTHER INFORMATION. The Chief Executive's office reports that it is 'absolutely inundated' with appeal letters of one kind or another.

NORWICH UNION INSURANCE GROUP

Surrey St
Norwich NR1 3NG   *Tel 0603 622200*

LOCAL ORGANISATION. Insurance branches all round the country.

POLICY. The Group donated £266,000 in 1988 (£236,000 in 1987) in the UK for charitable purposes. A fair proportion went to fund Nottingham University's chair of insurance. Besides the education field, donations are made to the medical field and to a mixture of national and local charities and appeals. Requests are judged against several criteria. For example, could policy holders benefit? (This is judged to be the case with donations to medical and educational charities). Could staff, of whom there are some 6,000, benefit? Would the donation benefit business? Is there an important customer of Norwich Union involved with the charity in question? What has Norwich Union done in the past with the charity? Is the Group acting as a 'good citizen' would if it were to provide support?

LOCAL GIVING. Requests going to branches are referred to head office, particularly those where local staff feel there is a good case for support, in order to coordinate donations. Sometimes regional offices, of which there are more than 35 across the country, will filter requests. £50,000 was given last year to a broad spectrum of voluntary groups in Norfolk and Suffolk.

OTHER INFORMATION. Appeals to head office should go to Mr D A Dorling, Assistant Company Secretary. In 1988 some 1,500 requests were received and the Group reports that it is a formidable job to sift the applications. It is very difficult to sift on a scientific basis, but the questions listed above are designed to help the sifting process.

PICKFORDS TRAVEL (See NFC PLC.)

PIZZA HUT UK LTD

Venture House
Hartly Avenue, Mill Hill
London NW7 2HX   *Tel 081-959 3677*

LOCAL ORGANISATION. 168 branches across the UK. Owned by Whitbread (see separate entry).

POLICY. No central budget held for giving cash to charities.

LOCAL GIVING. Normally local branches try to meet demand from local charities and give away vouchers for small amounts to be spent in branches.

OTHER INFORMATION. Head office contact should be made through the Marketing Dept.

THE POST OFFICE GROUP

33 Grosvenor Place
London SW1X 1PX   *Tel 071-235 8000*

LOCAL ORGANISATION. Three businesses (Letters, Parcels and Counters) are each divided into districts, with a district manager in each (64 for Letters, 12 for Parcels and 30 for Counters). Each district is centred on a major town across the UK. There are Post Office-owned counter offices, as well as franchised sub-offices.

POLICY. Charitable donations in 1988 amounted to £284,885. Policy and budgetting for charitable giving is decided from head office. The Board decides a charitable theme every three years, and until 1990 it is job creation and inner cities. This is the major budget. Cheques are often handed out by the district managers. There are regular annual donations to the Roland Hill Benevolent Fund, a staff association. There is a smaller budget for miscellaneous donations, usually to charities of a medical nature.

LOCAL GIVING. There is not much giving at the local level, but managers are being encouraged to get more involved in the community. Each district manager has a budget in the region of £1,000 annually and this is hoped to increase.

GIVING IN KIND. This is very rarely permitted, though there are exceptions such as free postage for receipt of donations for the Armenian earthquake.

STAFF ACTIVITIES. Staff are seconded and this policy is under review. At present staff are suspicious that secondment does not help their career prospects. Staff do fund raise and sponsor charities. Payroll giving has been in operation, and a new scheme is under discussion.

OTHER INFORMATION. The Post Office receives 20-30 requests nationally per week and the majority have to be turned down. One or two charities are reluctant to accept a negative answer, but by and large charities deal with them courteously. Appeals to head office should be addressed to the Deputy Secretary, Christina Lomas.

PRESTO STORES
(See Argyll Group PLC.)

PRUDENTIAL CORPORATION PLC

1 Stephen St
London W1P 2AP   *Tel 071-405 9222*

LOCAL ORGANISATION. One of the largest financial services groups with insurance offices and estate agencies nationwide.

POLICY. One percent of annual pre-tax profits goes to charities. In 1988 the Company and its subsidiaries made charitable donations of

£539,000 in the UK and £187,000 overseas. In the UK, financial support went to a wide range of organisations, including Education 2000, The Prince's Youth Business Trust, Business in the Community, and a broad cross-section of national and local projects in the fields of health and community welfare.

LOCAL GIVING. Much of the Company's giving is directed through a central Community Affairs Department within the Public Affairs Dept. There are 12 divisional offices and each will have a small budget for donations to charities. On the estate agency side, the divisional offices in theory have a budget for donations, but a more worthwhile approach would be for sponsorship of some kind. The Company's marketing people are always willing to consider proposals for support to charities providing there is a business return.

STAFF ACTIVITIES. The Company contributed an additional £370,000 in the UK through the secondment of 17 staff to organisations concerned with social issues, education and unemployment.

OTHER INFORMATION. Head office contact should be made through the Community Affairs Dept.

RATNERS GROUP PLC

19 Gt Portland St
London W1N 6HN   *Tel 071-580 9853*

LOCAL ORGANISATION. Jewellery retailers nationwide.

POLICY. Charitable donations totalled £60,103 in 1988. There is no set policy. Local managers direct all appeals to head office.

OTHER INFORMATION. Obtainable from the Chairman's office or Company Secretary.

ROYAL BANK OF SCOTLAND PLC

42 St Andrew Square
Edinburgh EH2 2YE   *Tel 031-556 8555*

LOCAL ORGANISATION. Banks throughout Scotland, as well as England-based offices.

POLICY. Head office deals with appeals from national charities. In 1988 the Group began to operate a Group Community Fund and made payments of £180,000 to organisations in communities throughout Gt Britain. The fund supports 'deserving causes' in three broad categories: job creation; the national heritage; and the environment.

LOCAL GIVING. Local appeals would be passed to the regional offices. There is at present no regional charity budget, though one is under consideration.

GIVING IN KIND. Branches occasionally display posters about charities and for charitable appeals in the branches. Collecting boxes are also sometimes put on counters, though this is judged on its merits.

STAFF ACTIVITIES. Bank branch staff are heavily involved in local charities.

OTHER INFORMATION. Appeals to head office should go to the Secretary. Sponsorship matters are dealt with by Mr G P Fenton, Public Relations Manager.

ROYAL INSURANCE HOLDINGS PLC

Corporate   Relations
1 Cornhill
London EC3V 3QR   *Tel 071-283 4300*

LOCAL ORGANISATION. Parent company of worldwide insurance group of 223 subsidiary companies and 30 associated companies with business in 80 countries through some 800 offices and more than 30,000 staff. Principal subsidiary companies in the UK are Royal UK (household insurance) and Royal Life (medical and life insurance) with main offices in Liverpool and Peterborough. The Company also controls a string of estate agencies trading under their own separate names (800 agency offices in total).

POLICY. The Company and its subsidiaries donated £495,300 in 1988 for charitable purposes with an additional £35,000 going to the Conservative Party. Worldwide, in 1988 the Company contributed £1,200,000 to 'community relations'. In the UK, the Company is a member of the Per Cent Club and contributed over £900,000 to 'the community', including the £495,000 quoted earlier 'for charitable purposes'. Contributions went to job creation, education and training and the arts. Other recent activities include property development projects in the inner cities and cash donations to charities. 70 charities received direct support.

LOCAL GIVING. In the UK, Royal Insurance employs over 4,000 people. The Company sponsored the production of pre-employment training booklets for all fifth and sixth year pupils on Merseyside. Royal UK and Royal Life were involved in 'Business Opportunities on Merseyside' which is concerned with urban regeneration. Support was also given to the local Wirral Association for the Disabled.

The Company is concerned with making links on a business footing with charities, national and local. To take Royal Life as an example, its Marketing Services Dept donates the commission for insurance business with Mersyside Regional Health Authority staff to the RHA. The Corporate Communications Manager is responsible for a good deal of 'community support activity' to local rather than national voluntary groups. His department welcomes good ideas from charities where Royal

Insurance can get a business return or publicity. Local managers have no local budget for direct giving, though they may provide some small support to local charities.

OTHER INFORMATION. Local charities are recommended to contact staff at head offices and to target their appeal if they believe there is a possible business return to the Company. The Company presently welcomes contact with schools and school children. If a charity is promising accreditation to the Company in a fund raising event or brochure, it should carry this through with the use of the Company's logo. The Company likes to increase the value of its giving through charity sponsorship. For example, an initial 'jail break' contribution of £1,500 to the Spastics Society led to £15,000 being raised when 60 local teams 'escaped' as far as possible in 24 hours.

SAFEWAY STORES
(See Argyll Group PLC.)

J SAINSBURY PLC
Stamford House
Stamford St
London SE1 9LL   *Tel 071-921 6000*

LOCAL ORGANISATION. One of Britain's largest food retailers with supermarkets nationwide. The Company owns the Savacentre hypermarket stores and the Homebase chain of DIY stores.

POLICY. Total 'community contributions' of £700,000 in 1988. Donations went to the arts, enterprise agencies, job creation and educational projects.

LOCAL GIVING. All giving is highly centralised. Usually, all appeals are sent to head office to ensure that there is no duplication. Small, local appeals can be dealt with if it is a question of a £5-25 gift voucher. There is a slightly different policy with outlets other than the supermarkets. Managers of Homebases currently have £25 monthly to allocate. Savacentres are larger units and may give more.

GIVING IN KIND. Area directors try to be helpful over such things as the use of supermarket car parks for such things as car boot sales for charity, or car wash services provided by the Scouts. Cash collections on the premises are generally limited to two per month, and to not more than once a year per charity. Charity 'trolley dashes' are permitted outside shopping hours. The Company may donate around £100 per minute, but the charity must meet the shopping bill.

STAFF ACTIVITIES. The whole of the retail division under the aegis of the Sainsbury Staff Association recently raised £350,000 for Macmillan Nurses. The cause is rotated every two years and determined at head office with local consultation.

OTHER INFORMATION. Head office charity post is very large, with some 400-500 letters per week. At Christmas the post is even heavier. What is tiresome is receiving the same letter from different branches of the same charity. Donations are channelled through the Sainsbury Charitable Fund, and appeals to head office should be addressed to the Secretary of the Fund.

SCOTTISH AIRPORTS LTD

St Andrew's Drive
Paisley
Renfrewshire
Scotland PA3 2ST   *Tel 041-848 4293*

LOCAL ORGANISATION. Part of BAA Plc. Airport operations in Glasgow, Edinburgh, Prestwick and Aberdeen.

POLICY. Support a whole range of Scottish and national charities. All requests are looked at by the Marketing Manager who operates a separate budget for charities. The Company pays special attention to advertising and promotional links with voluntary groups.

OTHER INFORMATION. The contact is Ms F McCusker. Following a recent reorganisation in the department concerned, a new strategy on charitable support is under discussion.

SCOTTISH AND NEWCASTLE BREWERIES PLC

111 Holyrood Rd
Edinburgh EH8 8YS   *Tel 031-556 2591*

LOCAL ORGANISATION. 2,300 pubs trading as William Younger (Southern England and Wales), Scottish and Newcastle (in Scotland and North East England), as well as Thistle Hotels. Major breweries in Edinburgh and Newcastle.

POLICY. Approximately i£200,000 in charitable donations made in 1988. No charities are ruled out for donations and all requests are considered. Charitable giving includes covenants. A charities committee meets four or five times per year.

LOCAL GIVING. All cash donations are made from head office. Products like beer would be donated locally for such things as raffle prizes. Charitable ventures in Edinburgh and Newcastle are particularly favoured.

OTHER INFORMATION. Appeals should go to Mr G B Reed, Board Director responsible for community affairs. Sponsorship is dealt with by Mr Iain McConnell.

SEARS PLC

40 Duke St
London W1A 2HP   *Tel 071-408 1180*

LOCAL ORGANISATION. Represented in the High St principally through footwear, men's and women's clothing shops, including Saxone, Dolcis, Freeman Hardy Willis, Trueform, Curtess, Shoe City (see separate entry for British Shoe Corporation), Selfridges, Miss Selfridge, Fosters, Dormie, Hornes, Milletts, Wallis, Adams.

POLICY. In 1988 £342,000 went in charitable donations. All the operating companies are instructed to divert appeals to the central

Sears Charitable Foundation. This has a fairly broad policy on giving. The bulk of the donations go to the major charities and 'fairly sizeable sums go to specialised charities that might produce worthwhile benefits'. 50 or 60 charities are supported, including those dedicated to research. The remainder of the money goes to smaller charities operating in specialist areas, mainly in the fields of the elderly, infirm, alchohol and drug abuse, and sporting activities.

LOCAL GIVING. The subsidiary companies give to local charities. But they largely give to trade-related charities, ie staff and ex-staff associations. Principally, these would be the Leicester-based British Shoe Corporation, Miss Selfridge and Fosters (Menswear).

OTHER INFORMATION. Appeals to head office should be addressed to Mr D J Ward.

SHELL UK LTD

Shell-Mex House
Strand
London WC2R 0DX   *Tel 071- 257 3000*

LOCAL ORGANISATION. The Company has major locations in Shell Haven, Essex, Stanlow, Cheshire and Aberdeen. There are PR managers in South East England, Midlands and Western, Northern England, Scotland and Northern Ireland, each approachable for support to local charitable activity.

POLICY. In 1988 charitable donations amounted to over £1 million. Community contributions of all kinds totalled £4.39 million. Nationally, Shell supports a wide range of charitable activities, including education, the arts, the environment (such as the Better Britain Campaign and Village venture) and enterprise. Policy on giving is business and community-related.

LOCAL GIVING. Besides the regional PR managers who each have a limited budget for charitable support, the Shell Community Service Fund of over £100,000 can be a source of limited amounts of money to local voluntary organisations in which Shell employees have an interest.

GIVING IN KIND. Giving is mostly in cash but giving in kind does sometimes take place through the donation of Shell publications such as the Shell Guide to Britain.

STAFF ACTIVITIES. Beside the Community Service Fund, there is staff secondment at national level (eg to the Nature Conservancy Council) and local level (eg an Essex enterprise agency). There is no payroll giving scheme.

OTHER INFORMATION. Mr K Guthrie, Grants Committee Secretary, at head office, deals with charity applications. Miss H M Barbour, Community Affairs Dept, deals with sponsorship matters.

SKETCHLEY PLC

Rugby Rd
Hinckley
Leicestershire LE10 2NE   *Tel 0455 38133*

LOCAL ORGANISATION. 500 branches throughout England and Wales.

POLICY. Giving is restricted to a small annual sum of £10,000 via the Sketchley Trust.

LOCAL GIVING. There is an annual round of consultation with staff and giving tends to go to small, local charities involving staff. Many of the charities are associated with some sort of disease or suffering. Small donations can be given of a few hundred pounds each. Staff consultation takes place early in the year and sums are paid out in the summer.

STAFF ACTIVITIES. Staff are too small in number at branch level to carry out much concerted effort, but staff at headquarters do carry out fund raising, for example, through car boot sales for a cancer unit at Leicester Royal Infirmary as well as fund raising for Leicestershire NSPCC.

OTHER INFORMATION. Miss D Harris is Secretary to the Sketchley Charitable Trust.

SKIPTON BUILDING SOCIETY

High St
Skipton
North Yorkshire BD23 1DN   Tel 0756 4581

LOCAL ORGANISATION. 57 branches across the country with a concentration in the North.

POLICY. The Building Society has no charitable budget for direct donations and considers that it is limited in the support it can give to charities. There is a central sponsorship budget and providing there is a business return to the Society, some assistance to charities can be given. The budget operates January to December and it is largely a question of 'first come, first served'. The budget is often fully allocated halfway through the year.

LOCAL GIVING. Local managers have a local advertising budget to work to and from this can sometimes provide sponsorship funds for local charities. Branches are equally interested in publicity for the Society. They can also provide a limited number of window displays for charity publicity.

OTHER INFORMATION. Mr T J Hughes, Marketing Manager, is the head office contact.

SOCK SHOP INTERNATIONAL PLC

180 Fleet St
London EC4A 2NT   Tel 071-627 8080

LOCAL ORGANISATION. Retailing of men's, ladies' and children's hosiery and fashion accessories. 104 outlets in the UK and a warehouse operation in Cambridgeshire. Also operates in USA and France.

POLICY. During the 17 months ending February 1989 the Company made charitable donations of £25,000. There is a Charitable Trust Fund to which charities can apply. Support is mainly given to the handicapped and disabled.

LOCAL GIVING. The charities supported tend to be London-based. Any request to a local outlet is passed to head office.

GIVING IN KIND. Discontinued fashion lines are donated.

OTHER INFORMATION. Head office contact through the chairman's office.

W H SMITH GROUP PLC

Strand House
7 Holbein Place
London SW1W 8NR   *Tel 071- 730 1200*

LOCAL ORGANISATION. Nationwide retailers of newspapers, books, stationery etc. in 400 High St outlets. Also over 100 Do It All DIY stores, 200 Our Price record retailing shops, 45 Sherratt and Hughes bookshops and 12 Paperchase specialised stationery stores. In 1989, the Company purchased the Waterstone chain of bookshops.

LOCAL GIVING. All appeals are sent to head office. Local managers have a very small budget for dealing with local requests, but the emphasis is upon 'very small'. Even requests for book vouchers find their way to head office. As some general donations are given to national headquarters of charities, appeals from their local branches are not considered, eg the Scouts. An awful lot of appeals come from the field of education. Requests from parent-teacher associations are now not generally considered.

STAFF ACTIVITIES. Locally, staff get involved in supporting charities. Nothing is laid down by way of company policy and activities tend to be ad hoc.

OTHER INFORMATION. The Company reports that it is inundated with appeals and head office receives some 25 to 30 letters each day. Appeals to head office should be directed to the Donations Secretary.

STANSTED AIRPORT LTD

Stansted
Essex CM24 8QW   *Tel 0279 502385*

LOCAL ORGANISATION. Part of BAA Plc (formerly the British Airports Authority). Large, expanding airport in eastern England.

POLICY. Policy similar to Gatwick Airport (see separate entry).

LOCAL GIVING. Operates a small local budget for small donations to local charities in the Essex area. The policy is to give small donations in order to spread support.

OTHER INFORMATION. Contact Mr C Hobbs, Head of Marketing.

STEAD AND SIMPSON PLC

Fosse Way
Syston
Leicester LE7 8PG   *Tel 0533 695981*

LOCAL ORGANISATION. 274 shoe retail outlets in Gt Britain. The Company also has some motor dealerships.

POLICY. In 1988 charitable donations totalling £5,700 were made. There is a policy on charitable contributions and a list of charities supported. The list includes charities associated with the shoe industry, particularly retired staff in the shoe industry. Some charities local to the Company's headquarters operation in Leicester receive covenants, and these have tended to be the choice of Directors of the Company. Over the past few years, a few new charities have been introduced to the list. The Company was recently taken over by Clayform Properties and policy may well change.

LOCAL GIVING. To Leicester-based charities where the Company is headquartered. All requests to branches are forwarded to head office. Collecting boxes in branches are not normally permitted.

STAFF ACTIVITIES. Left to the choice of the individual staff member.

OTHER INFORMATION. The Company wishes to point out that all appeals are considered on their merits. The head office contact is Mr S J Harvey, Company Secretary.

STOREHOUSE PLC

The Heal's Building
196 Tottenham Court Rd
London W1P 9LD   *Tel 071-631 0101*

LOCAL ORGANISATION. Represented nationwide through British Home Stores, Habitat, Mothercare, Richards.

POLICY. A considerable central budget for the major charities amounting to charitable donations in 1988 of £195,000. But apart from major covenants to major charities, the remaining budget for discretionary giving is very small. 'We try to help a few people properly', reports the Company.

LOCAL GIVING. In general, giving on a significant scale is not left to local store managers, though they might grant relatively small requests such as raffle prizes. Each chain of stores, however, will have slightly different policies on charitable giving.

OTHER INFORMATION. The Company reports that an 'incredible number of appeals letters are received every week' by head office. Appeals should be addressed to Ann Sayer, Group PR Manager.

SUN ALLIANCE INSURANCE GROUP

Bartholomew Lane
London EC2N 2AB
        Tel 071-588 2345

LOCAL ORGANISATION. Insurance offices nationwide. A major presence in Horsham where there are substantial administrative offices.

POLICY. In 1988 the Company and its subsidiaries gave £116,000 in the UK for charitable purposes. In addition, £40,000 was given to the Conservative Party and £6,000 to The Economic League. There is no firm policy on giving. The Company prefers to retain flexibility in policy. Donations are mainly made to the medical field and to medical research, the elderly and youth. There have been past donations to the RSPCA, NSPCC, Gt Ormond St Hospital and St Paul's Cathedral.

LOCAL GIVING. The Group's presence in Horsham means that charities there would receive special consideration. Local managers have little discretion to donate to charities and for the most part would pass correspondence to head office. Regional and local appeals are considered and funded where necessary – eg there is some funding of research at Cambridge's Addenbrooke's Hospital. But small, local appeals would not usually be considered without some special case being made out.

OTHER INFORMATION. Mr H Silver, Company Secretary, deals with charitable appeals.

SUPASNAPS (See Dixons Group Plc)

SUPERDRUG STORES PLC

40 Beddington Lane
Croydon
Surrey CR0 4TB   *Tel 081-684 7000*

LOCAL ORGANISATION. Part of Kingfisher PLC (see separate entry). A major High St retailer of chemist and related products. Fast recent expansion to a total of 600 outlets, including recent acquisition of Tip Top and Share Drug.

POLICY. The current charity 'adopted' by staff is the National Children's Home and most support is directed there.

LOCAL GIVING. Local managers cannot take any action so far as donating to local charities is concerned, or giving in kind. Most appeals are directed to head office or to supervisors who each take responsibility for ten stores.

OTHER INFORMATION. The company receives many appeal requests. The point of contact is Mrs Wright, Senior Associate Director, who heads up the Company's charity committee.

TESCO PLC

Tesco House
Delamere Rd
Cheshunt
Herts EN8 9SL   *Tel 0992 32222*

LOCAL ORGANISATION. Through Tesco stores and superstores nationwide. One of Britain's largest food retailers.

POLICY. £344,000 in charitable donations in 1988. All appeals are directed through the Tesco Charitable Trust. This operates independently of the Company and the trustees consider that it would be morally wrong for giving to be connected with Company policy.

LOCAL GIVING. Store managers are not empowered to give locally, either in cash or in kind, 'not even so much as a packet of chewing gum'. All applications are directed to head office and are considered on their merits. Some 3,000 small donations have been given in the past year and all are sifted according to their field of operation. The Company for the past three years has collected for the RNLI and has had a policy of allowing collections for age welfare organisations. It has also donated to children's charities, including Save the Children and the Variety Club. It places particular emphasis upon charities having low administrative costs. It favours handicapped children's organisations and those for the underprivileged. It also favours charities where the Company has a local outlet.

STAFF ACTIVITIES. Staff collect for charities on a prodigious scale, and they have raised, for example, considerable sums for Gt Ormond St Hospital. The Company runs a matching fund scheme which can add 20% on top of what is raised.

OTHER INFORMATION. The Company often receives multiple letters from the same charity and feels that charities really must co-ordinate their efforts. It feels that there is considerable duplication of effort between charities and far too many charities altogether. Mr John Eastoe is Director of Charities and Appeals.

TETLEY WALKER

The Brewery
Dallam Lane
Warrington
Cheshire WA2 7NU   *Tel 0925 31231*

LOCAL ORGANISATION. Part of Allied Lyons (see separate entry). Brewery operations in Liverpool, Blackpool, Kendal, Warrington.

POLICY. As a trading company within Allied Lyons, Tetley Walker operates the same policy on charitable giving. It supports a broad range of causes, particularly the handicapped, educational and young people, as well as other welfare-type charities. There is some giving to trade charities.

LOCAL GIVING. Within the budget specified by Allied Lyons, the Company favours charities local to its centres of operation. It would, for example, give to Oxfam locally. But a request from Oxfam, Oxford would be passed to a trading company within the Allied Lyons Group covering Oxford.

STAFF ACTIVITIES. Employees are involved in many local charities. Requests from staff for support to favourite charities are given special consideration.

OTHER INFORMATION. Appeals should be addressed to the Company Secretary.

TEXAS HOMECARE

Sywell Rd
Wellingborough   *Tel 0933 679679*

LOCAL ORGANISATION. Part of Ladbroke organisation. DIY retailers across the UK.

POLICY. A number of charitable causes are selected every year for the Company to donate to. The emphasis this year is upon youth and the National Association of Youth Clubs is the recipient charity.

LOCAL GIVING. Local managers receiving requests are asked to forward them to head office. Collecting boxes for the 'adopted' charity for the year are placed in local branches.

GIVING IN KIND. Takes place on a small scale. More often, assistance is provided to local charities through meeting fund raising requests of the kind which utilise company facilities, eg boy scouts being permitted to ask to clean customers' cars.

OTHER INFORMATION. Appeals to head office should be addressed to the Company Secretary.

THOMAS COOK

Thorpe Wood
Peterborough PE3 6SB   *Tel 0733 63200*

LOCAL ORGANISATION. 140 travel agencies across Britain. Owned by Midland Bank (see separate entry).

POLICY. The Company has a commitment to support charities, although present policy on support is under review. There is discussion on the possibility of supporting an as yet undisclosed charity.

LOCAL GIVING. The Company likes to support local charities particularly in its head office home town of Peterborough.

GIVING IN KIND. The Company does not give away holidays. It specialises in far-away destinations and these holidays are expensive to donate. Sponsorship of charitable events can be considered.

STAFF ACTIVITIES. The Company organises a major international running race for charity in Peterborough each June which raises 'an awful lot of money' for local charities.

OTHER INFORMATION. Obtainable through the Company Secretary's office.

THOMSON TRAVEL GROUP

Greater London House
Hampstead Rd
London NW1 7SD   *Tel 071-387 9321*

LOCAL ORGANISATION. Part of International Thomson Organisation. Thomson Travel includes Lunn Poly, one of the largest High St travel firms with 509 outlets in most major towns and cities.

POLICY. The policy is simple, reports the Company. Because the Company was inundated with requests, it decided in 1981, the

International Year for the Disabled, to support work providing holidays for the disabled. Almost the entire contribution from the Company goes to provide disability units for this purpose. The Company is involved with the Holiday Care Service and the Handicapped Aid Trust which provides funds for helpers with the handicapped. The Company does entertain applications for other funds, especially ones that are holiday-related.

LOCAL GIVING. Requests from local sources to local branches are passed to head office, sometimes routed through the Company's ten regional sales offices.

STAFF ACTIVITIES. Where staff do support a particular charity, and there are good grounds for Company support, this may be given in the form of a free holiday for a raffle prize.

OTHER COMMENTS. Mr R Wheal, Head of Consumer Affairs, heads up the policy committee on charitable support.

TIE RACK

2 Montpelier St
Knightsbridge
London SW7 1EZ   *Tel 081-995 134*

LOCAL ORGANISATION. Fast growing retailer of ties, scarves etc, including photographic and printing services. 125 UK outlets by 1989, with 86 overseas. It is the Company's intention to franchise the majority of its shops.

POLICY. No charitable or political donations were made in 1988. All appeals are passed to head office.

TOWN AND COUNTRY BUILDING SOCIETY

215 Strand
London WC2R 1AY   *Tel 071-353 1476*

LOCAL ORGANISATION. 250 branches and agencies in Britain. Administrative centre in Clacton-on-Sea.

POLICY. The Society can provide support to charitable organisations by way of indirect support through marketing and publicity. Local branch managers can make recommendations on charities to head office.

OTHER INFORMATION. Head office contact is Mr S Dilworth, Assistant General Manager, Marketing.

TRUSTHOUSE FORTE

166 High Holborn
London WC1   *Tel 071-836 7744*

LOCAL ORGANISATION. An international hotel and catering group. Hotels across the UK include THF, Post House and Anchor hotels. Catering includes Little Chef, Happy Eater, Welcome Break, Harvester Steak Houses and Falstaff Bars and Grills. Also runs London's Cafe Royal and Lillywhite's store, as well as public contract and in-flight catering.

POLICY. There is no set policy on giving, though youth and education are considered likely areas. There is no set limit on the amounts of individual donations. Some £555,000 was donated in all in the last financial year.

LOCAL GIVING. The Company does not exclude from giving to charities that are not national but can still be considered worthy of a donation. All appeals come to head office. If an appeal is of local interest to one of the Company outlets then the appeal papers will be sent from head office to the Company Secretary of the local division with a recommendation for a donation. There is a small divisional pot of money for divisions to dip into. Donations may be made from this, currently to a maximum of £150. Generally speaking, there are not a great deal of funds available locally. So far as the hotel outlets are concerned, if a charity is wanting use of, say, a hotel ballroom for a fund raising event, then an approach direct to the hotel manager might be worthwhile. Personal contacts are always useful. Sometimes at local level, raffle prizes are provided.

STAFF ACTIVITIES. There is no set policy. Locally, staff do get involved in charity fund raising, but they do so of their own accord.

OTHER INFORMATION. The Company reports that there are a great many appeals received from local schools. Head office is inundated with appeals from local branches of national charities, and these appeals are a waste of everybody's time. Appeals to head office should be addressed to Mr Tom Russell, Group Company Secretary.

TSB GROUP PLC

25 Milk St
London EC2V 8LU   *Tel 071-606 7070*

LOCAL ORGANISATION. An extensive national banking group, with the majority of branches in the North.

POLICY. TSB Group support for charities is through four TSB Foundations – for England and Wales, Scotland, Northern Ireland and the Channel Islands. For England and Wales in 1988/89, over £1.6 million went to 466 charities, on the basis of a 1% formula of profits donated. There are generally three different fields for giving – education and training, social and community needs and science and medical research. This last takes up large sums, committed over several years.

LOCAL GIVING. TSB favours applications in which it can give where it has a local presence. The Foundation likes to entertain applications from the North, in areas where the Bank has a strong presence. If appeals are received locally through a Bank branch, and if they are purely local, they will then go to the relevant regional office on the recommendation of the branch. It is possible to make an application direct to the Regional General Manager in the appropriate regional office, but again the application must be small and local in nature.

STAFF ACTIVITIES. Staff are involved in a great deal of local charity work, anything from participation in fun walks to bank managers acting as trustees for local charities. Staff time is not officially counted in as part of the Bank's charitable effort, but policy on encouraging staff to take part is being reviewed. Current support to the National Children's Home includes staff donating small sums and a matching grant from TSB. This is a pilot exercise that is likely to grow.

OTHER INFORMATION. Appeals to head office should be addressed to Mr R W Jenkins.

UNIGATE PLC

Western Avenue
London W3 0SH   *Tel 081-992 3400*

LOCAL ORGANISATION. Dairy and food distributers with locations across the country. Retail principally at the door.

POLICY. £97,000 in charitable donations in 1988. The Company does not want to encourage publicity about its charitable donations which are normally made on a long-term basis.

OTHER INFORMATION. Head office contact is Mr Nicholas Morris, Company Secretary.

VICTORIA WINE CO LTD

Brook House
Chertsey Rd
Woking   *Tel 04862 5066*

LOCAL ORGANISATION. Approximately 1,000 drinks retail outlets across the country. Part of Allied Lyons plc (see separate entry).

POLICY. Most large appeals are directed to Allied Lyons head office
which has its own separate trust for giving to charities on a large
scale. As a consequence, Victoria Wine does not normally contribute
to national charities on an annual basis.

LOCAL GIVING. In order to maintain central control over what
support Victoria Wine can offer, all appeals and correspondence are
dealt with from the Customer Services Dept at the Woking office,
and shops are requested to pass on appeals to this Department.
There is a central fund for charitable support, which runs into
thousands of pounds. But the Company has a policy of supporting
a large spread of appeals. Each appeal is replied to and giving is
usually of the order of a gift voucher of between £2 and £5.

GIVING IN KIND. Besides vouchers, shops are sometimes author-
ised to donate goods – bottles of wine usually – for charity raffles, etc.

OTHER COMMENTS. The Company receives on average around
200 appeals of one kind or another per week. Often, people who have
accounts in the shops and who ask for donations to their charities,
are helped.

OTHER INFORMATION. Appeals to head office should initially
go to the Company Secretary's office.

VIRGIN GROUP

95-99 Ladbroke Grove
London W11 1PG   *Tel 071-229 1282*

LOCAL ORGANISATION. A media production and retailing group, with travel interests. The Group has production facilities in the Notting Hill/ North Kensington area of London as well as a small chain of eight retailing outlets (Virgin Megastores) in the major cities. It is a series of independent companies, and approaches can be made to each part (eg Virgin Airlines) separately.

POLICY. Charitable donations of nearly £50,000 in 1988. The Group is proud of having no set policy. It reports that its charitable support is extensive at the national level, with support going to major national charities. There is a tie-up with Greenpeace, with 1% of nationwide earnings going to Greenpeace.

LOCAL GIVING. No set hard and fast policy. The group gives locally to voluntary organisations in the Notting Hill/ North Kensington area of London. Local charities approaching local outlets would normally get referred to head office.

GIVING IN KIND. Stores tend to give in kind where they deal with an application that is small in nature. In-kind giving would include such items as T-shirts, records, videos, games and computer games for raffles and other fund raising purposes.

OTHER COMMENTS. National contact can be made through Mr B Whitehorn, Head of Corporate Public Relations.

WHITBREAD & CO PLC

The Brewery, Chiswell St
London EC1Y 4SD   *Tel 071-606 4455*

LOCAL ORGANISATION. The Company has a major distribution centre at Wolverhampton and is also represented at local level in Magor, Gwent. It has smaller distribution centres in Cardiff and

Salford and a large subsidiary (Burroughs) in Glasgow. Besides the public houses owned by the Company, there are Threshers off-licences, Beefeater restaurants, Roast Inns, Brewers Fayre and Pizza Hut restaurants across the country. Managers of Beefeater outlets each have a small fund for giving and Pizza Hut operate their own policy (see separate entry).

POLICY. Over £400,000 in charitable donations were made in 1988. The Company divides appeals into seven categories, with sub-divisions in each category. They tend to make donations to the larger charities within each category, ignoring those which tend to be well-funded. The average donation is about £1,000. They sometimes take a gamble with smaller charities and will help with support at the early stages. They have large, existing commitments and they give to staff association charities in the brewing industry.

LOCAL GIVING. The Company likes to give to local areas in which it is represented. For example, it gave £25,000 to the Hillsborough Disaster Fund because it has a presence in the Liverpool and Manchester areas. Local managers might give out raffle prizes, but anything bigger has to be considered by head office.

COMMENTS ON APPEALS. Head office receives some 2,000 appeals each year, some of them very professionally done. The Company does not ignore photocopied appeals and sometimes considers that the 'shabbiest' looking document comes from the charity most in need. Every appeal is replied to. The one-page appeal is easiest to deal with, preferably accompanied with a set of accounts. Whitbread only give to registered charities.

OTHER INFORMATION. Mr P D Patten, the Board Charities Secretary, deals with appeals coming into head office.

WICKES PLC

19-21 Mortimer St
London W1N 7RJ   *Tel 081-863 5696*

LOCAL ORGANISATION. Retailer of home improvement products in 47 UK stores and 30 stores in continental Europe.

POLICY. The Group donated £30,122 to charities in 1988 and is a member of the Per Cent Club. Support went mainly to involvement with the Prince of Wales' Trust, and in particular to help with re-training programmes in Coventry. Small donations are also given, dealt with by head office.

LOCAL GIVING. All requests are dealt with by head office.

OTHER COMMENTS. Local charities are assisted, but enquiries in the first instance should be directed to Mr M Corner, Administration Director and Secretary to the Charities Committee.

WIGFALLS (See Dixons Group Plc.)

WOOLWORTHS

242 – 246 Marylebone Road
London NW1 6JL   *Tel 071-262 1222*

LOCAL ORGANISATION. Part of Kingfisher Plc (see separate entry). 780 stores across the country, retailing household goods.

POLICY. Woolworths 'adopt' a national charity each year and are heavily involved in charitable support at national level. The policy is one of encouraging staff to get involved across the country. Last year Woolworths sold £1.5 million worth of red noses in aid of Comic Relief, with some £100,000 going in donations from Woolworths alone. £276,000 went to 'Help a Child to See' in donations and fund raising by staff. The current emphasis is upon the National Children's Home, with a target figure to raise of £300,000.

LOCAL GIVING. Appeals to local managers would normally be sent to head office. Local managers have a small amount of discretion to give but this is something that the Company 'does not want to shout about'. Appeals directed to head office are numerous, with an average of 300 per week. The Company can only choose a small proportion of very deserving causes.

GIVING IN KIND. The small proportion of successful local appeals directed to head office cannot be sent cash. Usually, a prize for a raffle is sent. There is no sponsorship programme.

STAFF ACTIVITIES. See above. Staff are also heavily involved with supporting local charities, especially at Christmas time.

OTHER INFORMATION. Appeals to Woolworths should go in the first instance to the Company Secretary.

WOOLWICH EQUITABLE BUILDING SOCIETY

(See Gateway/Woolwich Equitable.)

YORKSHIRE BANK

20 Merrion Way
Leeds LS2 8NZ   *Tel 0532 441244*

LOCAL ORGANISATION. Some 250 branches as far south as Oxfordshire, east to Peterborough and as far north as South Shields.

POLICY. The Bank does make donations from head office, as well as delegating some responsibility to local branches. Donations in 1988 for charitable purposes amounted to £44,000. In addition, the Yorkshire Bank Charitable Trust contributed £66,000 to charitable organisations in the same year. The Bank actively supports local enterprise agencies, designed with training and employment in mind.

LOCAL GIVING. Local branches have their own budgets for supporting charities. This operates on an annual basis for giving small sums to local charities and for such things as sponsoring local charitable events. If a local charity is particularly favoured by local staff and the Bank feels it would want to be involved, then it would consider making a larger donation than permitted by the local budget. The Bank is most active in the Yorkshire region

STAFF ACTIVITIES. Staff are heavily involved in work with local charities.

OTHER INFORMATION. The Marketing Dept at head office deals with sponsorship matters at national and regional level. Sponsorship has included theatrical and musical events in Sheffield and York. The Bank is active in schools and running school programmes such as inter-school swimming and cross-country events and it operates mobile units for banking purposes at shows and exhibitions. Appeals to head office should be routed through the Secretary's office.

INDEX

114

Directory of Social Change
Company Giving Books

The Directory of Social Change publishes a wide range of publications on company giving. These include:

- **A Guide to Company Giving**
  Details of 1300 top companies and how they give to charity.

- **Major Companies and their Charitable Support**
  A detailed look at the donations and community involvement policies of the top 350 companies.

- **Raising Money from Industry**
  A practical guide to approaching companies.

- **Finding Sponsors for Community Projects**
  A step-by-step guide to getting sponsorship for social, environmental, community and other projects.

- **A Guide to Community Award Schemes**
  A survey of the many competitions and award schemes which offer cash prizes for community and environmental projects.

- **Company Giving News Service**
  A three-times a year news service with the facts and figures of company giving.

For details of prices and latest editions, write to the Directory of Social Change, Radius Works, Back Lane, London NW3 1HL.

Directory of Social Change
Grant Guides

The Directory of Social Change publishes a wide range of grant guides for charities. These include:

- **A Guide to the Major Trusts**
  Details of the background, donations policies, grant programmes and application procedures of around 450 large trusts in the UK.

- **A Guide to Company Giving**
  Details of 1300 companies and how they give to charity.

- **Major Companies and their Charitable Support**
  A detailed look at the community involvement policies of the top 350 companies.

- **The Central Government Grants Guide**
  A guide to grants for central government departments, official bodies authorized to distribute government money and grant funds administered by voluntary organisations on behalf of government.

- **A Guide to Grants for Individuals in Need**
  Details of 1500 trusts and other sources which make grants to individuals for the relief of need and distress.

- **The Educational Grants Directory**
  Around 1500 trusts and other sources which make grants to individuals in need for educational purposes.

- **The London Grants Guide**
  A guide to local, statutory, trust and company grant sources with specific local grant-making policies in the Greater London area.

- **Environmental Grants**
  A guide to statutory, trust and company grants for environmental purposes.

- **Peace and Security**
  A guide to grant sources (UK and overseas) and independent organisations in the field of peace, security and international relations.

For details of prices and latest editions, write to the Directory of Social Change, Radius Works, Back Lane, London NW3 1HL.

The Directory of Social Change

The Directory of Social Change is an educational charity established in 1975. It is based in London and has a Northern Office in Merseyside. It aims to promote the effective use of charitable resources. It does this by:

> Publishing a range of grant guides, advisory handbooks and information sources on all aspects of fundraising and charity management.

> Organising a national programme of training courses in fundraising, financial management, communication skills, management skills and personal skills. These courses are aimed exclusively at charities and voluntary organisations.

> Organising conferences and seminars on matters of current interest.

> Undertaking and publishing research.

> Developing pilot initiatives.

Further information from the Directory of Social Change, Radius Works, Back Lane, London NW3 1HL (071-435 8171).